Building Solidarity with the Grenada Revolution

by Andrew Pulley

[The following report was presented August 11 to an expanded meeting of the Socialist Workers Party Political Committee. It was adopted unanimously by the Political Committee on August 13, 1980.]

* * *

The actions of the People's Revolutionary Government of Grenada, its pro-worker and anti-imperialist policies, leave no doubt in our minds that we have the first workers and farmers government of Black and English-speaking people anywhere in the world.

This fact has deep ramifications not only for the revolution in the Caribbean and Latin America, but also for the struggles of working people in the United States.

This was evident to Steve Clark, Diane Wang, and me when we visited Grenada earlier this summer. We witnessed firsthand the heritage of poverty and misery created by imperialism. We learned about the concrete steps being taken in education and health care to improve the lives of the Grenadian people. Everywhere we went, we saw signs of the internationalism of this revolution—from the poster of Che Guevara in front of Barclay's bank, to the lessons about internationalism being taught in the schools.

Most importantly, we saw how the masses are being organized and politically educated, how unions and other mass organizations are being built, how the participation of the masses is key to the forward march of the revolution. And we could not help but think of what an example this will be for workers' struggles in the United States.

We also learned new facts about how imperialism is trying to crush this revolution. Prime Minister Maurice Bishop told us that ex-dictator Eric Gairy is trying to recruit mercenary forces, including Black Americans from Miami, to attack the revolution. This goes on while the U.S. government refuses to honor Grenada's offical request that Gairy be extradited. The harboring of this criminal is a symbol of the U.S. government's continuing support to counterrevolution, attempted assassinations, coup attempts, and other terrorist attacks against the revolution.

The U.S. government has big stakes in the Caribbean. There are 30 million people in the Caribbean, with nearly 90 percent of them in six countries: Cuba, Puerto Rico, the Dominican Republic, Haiti, Jamaica and Trinidad. As of 1977, American imperialism had about 4.5 billion dollars invested in this area, and that's not including Puerto Rico.

The United States is extremely concerned about the impact of the Grenadian example throughout the Caribbean and Latin America. Within days of the March 13 insurrection, there were rallies in solidarity with Grenada in Barbados, Guyana, Jamaica, and elsewhere. Informal political links also exist between the New Jewel Movement and political organizations on other islands.

The U.S. government is also concerned about the potential impact of the Grenadian revolution on Blacks and working people in this country. There has always been a relationship between the Black struggle in the Caribbean and the Black struggle in the United States. This goes back to the Garvey movement in the 1920s, and back even further, to the fight against slavery. We have the same roots in the rebellions against slavery in the 19th century. More recently, Black Power movements in Trinidad and elsewhere interacted with the Black Power movement in the United States. We found out, for example, that one of the heroes of the leaders of the New Jewel Movement was Malcolm X. We also found out that Malcolm X's mother was from Grenada. There are many Grenadians, and other West Indians, who live in the United States.

We can be sure that when Blacks in the United States begin to learn what the Grenadians are doing, they are going to be inspired. The Black youth fighting today against police terror, fighting for jobs and simple human dignity, are going to want to emulate the Grenadian example.

Unionists are also going to be inspired by a government that is pro-union, that supports the building of unions. American women will prefer the Grenadian way when they hear that Grenadian women are becoming equal in law and fact. And masses of Americans, facing inflation and high taxes, will be interested to learn how Grenada has lifted all taxes from the lowest paid 30 percent of the workforce, while slapping big taxes on the capitalists.

All the gains being made by the Grenadian revolution are going to have an impact internationally. And that is why the U.S. government has been completely hostile to this revolution from the very beginning. Right after the revolution, the U.S. government considered the possibility of a naval quarantine. And although they did not follow through on this, they did begin a big campaign about the supposed violation of human rights and free press in Grenada. *U.S. News and World Report* ran a big article on the "Serpent in the Caribbean Paradise." And, of course, Grenada was one of the objects of the "Solid Shield 80" maneuvers planned for the spring, and of the phony Soviet combat brigade crisis whipped up by Carter last fall.

They have also begun to coldly apply economic pressure. American oil firms cut back oil shipments, causing power shortages in the early days of the revolution. And they began a concerted campaign to sabotage tourism, warning American tourists that Grenada was too dangerous a place to go, spreading wild stories about supposed Soviet missile bases in Grenada, Cuban tanks occupying the streets, and so forth.

We can expect that all these efforts to sabotage the revolution will continue. We can expect that the U.S. imperialists will continue to be 100 percent opposed to the progress being made by the workers and farmers of Grenada. And this makes all the more clear to us the great importance of building a solidarity movement in defense of the Grenadian revolution in the United States.

A strong solidarity movement here can make a difference in whether this promising new revolution can survive in the face of U.S. threats. And a strong solidarity movement can also play a big role in getting out the truth about this revolution to the American masses, in holding up the Grenadian revolution as an example of how to struggle, of how real gains can be won by working people.

There are two distinct aspects of the activities we will be carrying out in defense of the Grenadian revolution. First, we will be using our election campaign, our newspaper, and other publications to get out the truth about the revolution. Second, we will be joining hands with other groups and individuals to build a broad movement in solidarity with the Grenadian revolution.

You may have noticed in the interview we had with Maurice Bishop [See pg. 25] that he mentioned our party's efforts to get out the story of Grenada through the *Militant*. He pointed in particular to the importance of getting out information showing concretely how the revolution was meeting the basic needs of the population—how it was bringing gains in jobs, health, housing, food and so forth.

Through this fall's *Militant* subscription drive, *Young Socialist* sales drive, through our 1980 election campaign, and through our forums, we can reach many more people with the story of the revolution. As soon as I returned from Grenada, for example, I was interviewed by all the major Black newspapers in New York—the *Amsterdam News*, *Big Red* (which has the largest circulation), and the *Black American*. Articles have already appeared in the *Amsterdam News* and *Big Red*. And more interviews with radio stations can be lined up when I return for the Caribbean Day events in Brooklyn on Labor Day.

Half a million to a million people from all of the Caribbean islands traditionally parade in Brooklyn on Labor Day. We are projecting a big participation in that event with our emphasis being on getting out news of the Grenadian revolution and answering the lies of the counterrevolutionaries. Comrades from other branches on the East Coast are being asked to help out.

Earlier this year, New York held a *Militant* forum on Grenada addressed by a representative from the Grenadian Consul General's office. Last year Brother Kendrick Radix, Grenada's U.N. Ambassador, spoke at a *Militant* forum on Blacks and the PLO. So, if your branch has not already had a forum on Grenada, you will probably want to schedule one.

Along with these activities, we also want to unite with as many other individuals and groups as possible to build a broad solidarity movement.

A U.S.-Grenada Friendship Society has been formed. Last April, 200 people attended a founding national conference of this group in Washington, D.C. Thus far, the committee has not carried out much activity, but the conference did project a national newsletter, speaking tours, and material aid collections.

The Grenadians are anxious to see this solidarity movement grow. Maurice Bishop mentioned it in the interview.

Most cities do not at this time have U.S.-Grenada Friendship Societies. In fact, as far as I know, they only exist in a few cities. But this should not stop us from getting started right away on this solidarity work. We should get rolling now on organizing activities that will interest people in Grenada, that will attract activists who will want to help us build a unit of the U.S.-Grenada Friendship Society in every city.

There are many different kinds of activities that can get a solidarity movement off the ground. Someone can prepare a talk on Grenada and present it on a campus, at a union hall, before a Black community organization, or perhaps a church. Or you can begin by getting a group of people together more informally, in someone's home. One thing we can use in these initial gatherings is the tape we have here of the speech made by Maurice Bishop on the night of the June 19 bombing and attempted assassination of the Grenadian leadership.

For larger meetings, speakers can be gotten by writing to the Consul General, Permanent Mission of Grenada, 141 East 44th Street, Room 905, New York, N.Y. 10017.

We should also be mindful that a number of comrades have already been to Grenada and are able to speak about it.

We want to take a bold approach. We think there will be many, many people who will want to hear about this revolution. We want to take this campaign into the unions, to Grenadian workers we work with (as comrades have already been doing at the Brooklyn Navy Yard), to Black workers and to workers in general. We want to try to speak about this in front of unions, to get unions and labor officials to support calls for material aid.

We want to get endorsements of the U.S.-Grenada Friendship Society, and participation where possible, from prominent Blacks, labor figures, and activists in the womens' movement. Black groups such as the NAACP, PUSH, and the All African Revolutionary Peoples' Party, as well as Black churches, Black student groups, and unions that are heavily Black will all have a special interest in this campaign.

Rev. Herbert Daughtry of the Black United Front has already visited Grenada, and we can expect other leaders of the Black and union movements to do the same. One of the prominent speakers at the recent PUSH convention was Dessima Williams, Grenada's representative to the Organization of American States.

We will also be working with members of the Communist Party and other radicals in this effort. Members of the CP have already played a big role in the U.S.-Grenada Friendship Society where it has been set up.

We should encourage our co-workers and all those who might be interested, including prominent individuals, to visit Grenada. This is something that is stressed by the New Jewel Movement. They say, "Come on down and see for yourself." There is no better way to inspire people about the revolution and to cut through the lies than to have people see for themselves. And each of these visitors becomes a potential propagandist for the revolution.

We should also help counter the attempts of the U.S. government to sabotage the tourist industry. Many of the tourists who presently vacation in Grenada are not of the same class that our party is orienting to. They go down on "love boats," etc. But, nevertheless, the income from this tourism is important to Grenada's economy, and we should expose and oppose any efforts to hurt it.

We should also encourage those workers who are able to afford it to take vacations in Grenada. The People's Revolutionary Government has said they hope that more working-class people, more Blacks, will now come to take vacations in Grenada, which is said to be the most beautiful island in the Caribbean. In order to go to Grenada, you do not need a visa, you do not even need a passport (although it is better if you have one), and you do not have to go on any special tours. You can just go.

The U.S.-Grenada Friendship Society can play a big role in countering the lies being spread against Grenada by the counterrevolutionaries. The *Militant* will be helping with this. For example, we will soon be carrying an article answering the lies of Curtis Stuart, the ex-head of Grenada's Technical and Allied Workers Union, who turned against the revolution. Stuart recently slandered free Grenada in an interview with the publication *Free Trade Union News,* which is put out by the Meany-inspired American Institute for Free Labor Development, notorious for its collaboration with the CIA against the Latin American labor movement.

The Friendship society will also be gathering material aid for Grenada and demanding that the U.S. government send aid. We will have to get more information on what specific projects the Grenadians want money for, but we can be sure that any funds we can gather will be welcome. Fundraising is an activity that many different groups and individuals can become involved in. We can get union contributions, have collections in the plants, get students raising money, churches, etc. The Canadians, who have raised over $2 million for Nicaragua, can provide an example.

Something we can look forward to will be more meetings, or possibly a tour, by representatives of the New Jewel Movement or the union movement in Grenada. We, of course, would want to build meetings as broad as possible for such speakers—with sponsors, funds raised, honoraria, etc.

Units of the U.S.-Grenada Friendship Society should subscribe to the *Free West Indian,* the weekly newspaper in Grenada. And we should sell subscriptions to this newspaper to all who are interested. Already at this Oberlin conference, some sixty subscriptions were sold.

As soon as solidarity activities begin to get organized, reports on them should be sent to the U.S.-Grenada Friendship Society, as well as the Grenada Mission to the U.N. in New York, and the Ministry of Information in Grenada. The addresses are:

1. U.S.-Grenada Friendship Society
   c/o Permanent Mission of Grenada
   141 East 44th Street
   Room 905
   New York, N.Y. 10017

2. Permanent Mission of Grenada
   141 East 44th Street
   Room 905
   New York, N.Y. 10017

3. Ministry of Information
   Prime Minister's Office
   Belmont, St. George's
   Grenada

One thing we will find is that Nicaraguan solidarity work and Grenadian solidarity work will interrelate. Those who are supporting the Nicaraguan revolution will want to support Grenada. And the same thing will be true of supporters of the Cuban revolution.

We also know that activists in the antidraft movement will be especially interested in finding out about the revolutions in the Caribbean. The movement against the draft is one of the best ways to defend the Grenadian, Nicaraguan, and Cuban revolutions. Supporters of these revolutions will also be antidraft.

It is hard now to totally envision all the possibilities of Grenadian solidarity work, but we know they will be great. We also cannot overestimate the importance of this work, of defending and building support for this revolution.

As we carry out this activity, as we counter and mess up the plans of the imperialists, as we inspire working people with the example of the Grenadian revolution, there is something else that will happen that is of great importance. Marxism will begin to become more of a Black thing in this country. We will begin to see more Blacks looking to Marxism for answers, because they are inspired by a revolution that is guided by the ideas of Marxism.

And we can expect to find many people—Blacks, whites, Chicanos, Puerto Ricans, students and workers—who will, as a result of learning about the Grenadian revolution, want to fight for a revolution in the United States. And many will want to join the revolutionary movement in this country.

We can look to the example of the New York Young Socialist Alliance, where solidarity with the Nicaraguan revolution and other activities has led to a YSA of over fifty members, many of them Spanish-speaking. We should look forward to "Two, three, many New York YSAs." That should be our goal.

Grenada: A Workers and Farmers Government with a Revolutionary Proletarian Leadership

by Steve Clark

[The following report was presented August 10 to an expanded meeting of the Socialist Workers Party Political Committee. It was adopted unanimously by the Political Committee August 13, 1980.]

* * *

The new government of Grenada is a workers and farmers government with a revolutionary proletarian leadership, the New Jewel Movement (NJM). That is what all the evidence demonstrates. We need to assess this step forward in the world revolution and its significance for our movement both in this country and internationally.

We must fully absorb the implications of this revolutionary victory and the caliber of its leadership. Its importance for the entire Caribbean, especially the countries with predominantly Black populations—Jamaica, Haiti, Guyana, Barbados, Trinidad and Tobago, Martinique, Guadeloupe, St. Vincent, St. Lucia, Dominica, Antigua, and other islands.

And we need to grasp its importance for Blacks and for *all workers* here in the United States, Canada, and Britain in particular.

This is true not only in order to help orient our activities in solidarity with Grenada, but because of the intransigently class-conscious and internationalist example that this "big revolution in a small country"—as Fidel Castro aptly described it—can set for Blacks and other working people in our own country.

The Grenada revolution is an integral part of the revolutionary rise throughout the Caribbean and Central America. The Grenadians explain that without the Cuban revolution, there could have been no free Grenada, there could have been no free Nicaragua. And together with the Nicaraguans and Cubans, they see themselves as part of a revolutionary triangle. If the imperialists "touch Cuba or if they touch Nicaragua, then they touch Grenada too" is the way Prime Minister Maurice Bishop put it at the massive 1980 May Day rally in Havana.

When Comrade Liam James from the New Jewel Movement spoke at the Caribbean solidarity rally here a week ago, he pointed out that without the existence of the Soviet Union, there could have been no Cuban socialist revolution twenty years ago, and without revolutionary Cuba there would be no revolutionary Grenada today. We should think about this, it's important. Because the key for Grenada—given its size, its location, and the particular political and economic problems it faces—is the Cuban revolution. Of course, Grenada is seeking aid from the Soviet Union, as from all economically powerful countries, and we hope it gets every bit as much as it needs. But the *key* question for the survival and development of free Grenada is Cuba's internationalist foreign policy and the extension of the socialist revolution throughout Central America and the Caribbean.

We first began to take serious notice of the Grenada revolution last fall, when its leaders stood up to imperialism at the Non-Aligned Conference and during Carter's fake crisis around the "Soviet combat brigade." We noticed that Prime Minister Maurice Bishop was the first person to rush to the podium and embrace Fidel Castro after his scathing indictment of imperialism before the United Nations General Assembly.

So in late October 1979, we sent Ernie Harsch down to see what was going on and to report on it for *Intercontinental Press* and the *Militant*. And we sent Jerry Hunnicutt back down for the first anniversary celebration of the revolution in March. Most recently, Andrew Pulley, Diane Wang, and I spent a week there, talking to working people and to leaders of the mass organizations, government, and NJM, and receiving frank, lengthy interviews, including one from Prime Minister Bishop.

So we've been able to develop a good feel for and body of knowledge about this revolution, which we've sought to communicate through expanded coverage in the press of our movement. As revolutionists, we've taken the opportunity in Grenada—as we've done in Nicaragua—to follow close-up the development of a revolution and its leadership, and to begin learning everything we can from these rich, class-struggle experiences.

Based on this information, this report is divided into two parts. The first will briefly go over some highlights of the history of the New Jewel Movement and of the struggle in Grenada; the reaction to the Grenadian revolution by imperialism; its impact on the peoples of other Caribbean islands and in Cuba and Nicaragua; some facts about the class structure and economy of Grenada and the problems they pose for the revolution; and the accomplishments and challenges before the revolutionary leadership.

Drawing on this background, the second part of the report will examine the character of the government and its leadership.

The Road to Revolution

The deposed dictator Eric Gairy rose to prominence in Grenada at the beginning of the 1950s as the founder and leader of the Grenada Mental and Manual Workers Union. This was mainly an agricultural workers union, the first important union on the island. It conducted militant strikes and demonstrations against the big landowners and British colonialists. Thus Gairy became a national hero, a symbol of the struggle against British colonialism in that period.

Under the pressure of these events and of the rise of the colonial revolution worldwide, the British rulers began to seek a neocolonial solution to maintain their grasp on Grenada. And Gairy bought right into the offer, using his influence to build a political base and to enrich himself. He became a member of the Chamber of Commerce and bought large tracts of land and commercial enterprises. As he gained more and more political power, he used it—much as Somoza did in Nicaragua—to boost his own profits and properties at the expense of other capitalists. Gairy initially served as premier while the island was still a British possession, and he remained in that post following formal independence in 1974. During twenty-three years of his rule, he drove not only masses of workers and farmers into opposition to his dictatorial regime, but growing layers of the Grenadian bourgeoisie, as well.

The New Jewel Movement arose in 1973 out of a fusion of two organizations—the Movement for the Assembly of Peoples (MAP), and the Joint Effort for Welfare, Education, and Liberation (JEWEL). Its initial leaders remain central leaders of the New Jewel Movement and People's Revolutionary Government (PRG) today—individuals such as Selwyn Strachan; Unison Whiteman; Kendrick Radix, now the ambassador to the United States and United Nations; and the current prime minister, Maurice Bishop.

The NJM developed out of the Black Power movement in the Caribbean in the early 1970s, as did Walter Rodney and many other anti-imperialist fighters and radical political currents throughout the Caribbean. This trend was profoundly influenced both by the Black struggle in the United States and figures ranging from Martin Luther King to Malcolm X, and by its identification with the Cuban revolution and its leaders, such as Fidel and Che.

The NJM went through an important further programmatic and political development in the seven years after its founding. The class struggle began affecting it more deeply and directly. That process is described in the interview that Ernie Harsch conducted last October with Selwyn Strachan, one of the central leaders of the New Jewel Movement and minister of labor, works, and communications [see appendix I for full text].

Strachan told Ernie that at the outset, the New Jewel Movement was "a revolutionary democratic party. We never called ourselves socialist at the beginning."

But the NJM had a very radical program: land reform; state control of foreign trade; eventual nationalization of the banks, insurance companies, and tourism; a program to make the country more self-sufficient in food; improving the schools, upgrading health, and so on.

Over time, Strachan said, the New Jewel Movement began to explicitly view itself, "As a socialist party, with the objective of bringing socialism to this country."

"As we got more and more mature," he told Ernie, "we were able to work out a clearer ideological position. It didn't come artificially, it was a result of struggle, in a concrete way."

One of the first major class-struggle experiences that the New Jewel Movement went through was the massive and prolonged upsurge during the last half of 1973 and early 1974. This upsurge almost succeeded in bringing down the Gairy regime.

At the time, the NJM was still a young organization. It was beginning to win mass support and held a rally of 10,000 at one point during the upsurge. But it had little or no base in the Grenadian working class and had not yet fully developed its current understanding of the workers as the leading class force in the revolution.

At the beginning of 1974, the NJM called for a general strike. A militant six-week strike did occur; to Gairy's consternation, it continued right through the February 7 ceremonies marking Grenada's formal independence from Britain. But at the head of the striking unions were reformist officials who were members of the bourgeois Grenada National Party, which was also supporting the strike, along with the Chamber of Commerce and Employers' Association.

Just at the point where the Gairy regime was on the verge of toppling, these bourgeois figures and class-collaborationist union leaders looked over their shoulders. They were frightened by what they saw—the growing influence of the NJM, the workers in a fighting mood, a situation potentially out of their control. So they reined in the workers, called off the strike, and the first big opportunity to bring down Gairyism was missed.

The NJM drew some conclusions from this sell-out, and it had further experiences with the Grenada National Party, too. In the 1976 elections, the NJM formed an anti-Gairy electoral alliance with the GNP and the conservative United People's Party. Despite Gairy's rigging, the NJM ended up winning three seats, and Bishop became the official leader of the parliamentary opposition, remaining so until the insurrection.

After the 1976 election, according to Strachan, the NJM drew the conclusion that the GNP and UPP "were not useful at all. They were more of a political liability than anything else."

Instead of orienting towards these bourgeois opposition forces, the NJM increasingly turned its efforts toward building a base among the urban and rural workers. It began to organize and prepare for the revolutionary action that it knew would be necessary to bring down the Gairy regime and mobilize the masses in order to be able to implement the NJM program.

So NJM leaders organized the Bank and General Workers Union. They began getting active in other major unions—the teachers union, the Commercial and Industrial Workers Union, the dock workers union. Their aim was to win the political leadership of the Grenadian workers away from the GNP, so that the power of the working class could be mobilized to bring down Gairyism and begin rebuilding society on a new basis.

Comrades who have read the articles in *IP* and the *Militant,* already know that a hard-fought NJM-led strike against Barclay's Bank in late 1978 and early 1979 helped set the stage for the revolution.

In March 1979, NJM leaders discovered that Gairy was planning to arrest and execute them. On the morning of March 13 they organized a group of forty-six people, took over the True Blue army barracks, went to the radio station, and put out a call to the masses of Grenada to come into the streets. And the masses responded, with the workers in the lead as the decisive component of the popular uprising. They marched on the police stations, and by the end of the day the corrupt and rotten Gairy regime had crumbled. The People's Revolutionary Government had come to power.

The Response Abroad

What was the response of U.S. imperialism?

It was extremely alarmed about this revolution, and it had good reason to be. It recognized the impact Grenada would have throughout the whole Caribbean, and the example it could set for Blacks and other working people in the United States. Most important of all, it also quickly discovered that it was dealing with a principled revolutionary leadership—one built along the lines of the Castro team—that was committed to the world revolution, not to deals with U.S. imperialism at the expense of the world's toilers.

The impact in the Caribbean region revealed itself immediately. In the discussion period, Gilbert [Pago, of the Socialist Revolution Group (GRS), Antilles section of the Fourth International] has offered to give us a bit of a feel for the explosive tremors in this whole chain of Caribbean islands during the days and weeks directly following the March 13 revolution. [An interview with Gilbert Pago appears as Appendix III.]

Andrew [Pulley] in his report on solidarity work will go into a few of the details on how the U.S. government has expressed its hostility toward the Grenada revolution: the military pressures, the economic sabotage, the barrage of lies and rumors about the revolution.

Behind all these moves is the U.S. rulers' hatred of the Cuban revolution. They fear the example of the Cuban revolution. They despise another step forward in the socialist revolution, in this hemisphere. And they fear the inspiring appearance of another internationalist leadership, part of the broader Marxist current that the Cuban victory and experiences originated.

Washington's deep hostility was compounded several months after the Grenada revolution by the Sandinista victory in Nicaragua, and by the spur this gave to revolutionary developments in El Salvador, Guatemala, Honduras, and elsewhere in Central America.

Only one month after the NJM took power, the U.S. ambassador to Grenada and nearby Barbados, Frank Ortiz—who is now ambassador to Guatemala!—gave a message to the PRG that the U.S. government "would view with displeasure any tendency on the part of Grenada to develop closer ties with Cuba."

The PRG's response came that very night in a radio address by Bishop. "We are not in anybody's backyard," he said, "and we are definitely not for sale." The next day formal diplomatic relations were announced between Grenada and Cuba.

Since that time, the Grenadian revolutionists have proven that they aren't in anyone's backyard. They proved it by their firm stance against imperialism at the Non-Aligned Conference in the fall, by their speeches and votes in the United Nations, and by their public pronouncements in solidarity with international freedom struggles. Despite its small size, vulnerability, and need for aid, Grenada is definitely not for sale.

What was the impact elsewhere in the Caribbean? The governments most closely tied to U.S., British, and French imperialism have been openly hostile. These include the governments of Trinidad, Barbados, and other islands.

On the other hand, the Grenadian revolution has inspired the toiling masses of these countries and had a profound impact on political groups and trade unions throughout the Caribbean.

To illustrate both sides of this situation, Gilbert will report on the impact in Martinique and Guadeloupe and how the French imperialists responded by bringing in thousands of troops both aimed against Grenada and at the workers of these two French colonies. There are now more than 16,000 French troops stationed there!

The Cuban and Nicaraguan leaderships, of course, have had a totally different response. They have embraced the New Jewel Movement as fellow revolutionists, as part of their current. Fidel calls Grenada, Nicaragua, and Cuba the "three giants on imperialism's doorstep."

Bishop was a featured speaker at the big May Day rally in Havana. He has already been invited to Nicaragua twice—to speak at the Carlos Fonseca celebration in February and at the giant July 19 first anniversary celebration just a few weeks ago.

Grenada has received massive aid from Cuba. The Cubans have contributed 100 pieces of heavy earth-moving machinery and trucks worth EC$25 million [East Caribbean $1=U.S.$0.38] to build Grenada's new international airport, along with 250 technicians and workers to help construct it and to train Grenadians to complete the construction. The Cubans have also donated many scholarships, thirteen doctors and dentists (doubling the number on the island), and twelve fishing trawlers so Grenada can begin a fishing industry.

The next largest aid package so far has come as a combined grant of $27 million from the governments of Algeria, Syria, and Libya.

The USSR has pledged EC$3 million in agricultural equipment.

Economy Distorted by Imperialism

Because of centuries of colonial and then neocolonial imperialist domination, Grenada has been left with an extremely distorted capitalist economy. You see the devastating results when you go down there to visit—very, very graphically. You see the poverty, brutal imperialist refusal to allow development; the poor roads, inadequate housing—and the stark contrast with the tourist enclaves.

In his speech at the Havana Non-Aligned Conference, Prime Minister Bishop spoke about the particular problems faced by Grenada and other "small island and specially disadvantaged states."

These problems, he said, include "limited markets, limited populations, limited resources, lack of skills in key areas, heavy dependence on one or two raw materials for export earnings, lack of capital formation, undeveloped money markets and inadequate infrastructure." Such problems, he pointed out, affect not only Grenada, but small countries such as Dominica and St. Lucia in the Caribbean, and the Seychelles and São Tomé off the coast of Africa.

These very small countries, Bishop said, are "doubly hit by imperialism. Whereas the larger countries of the Third World are today fighting for the right to achieve a better balance in their terms of trade, for many of us the fight is for the right to trade in the first place."

The main sources of foreign exchange earnings for Grenada are agriculture and tourism. Its main agricultural exports are nutmeg, cocoa, and bananas, along with other fruits and spices.

Tourism is the second largest source of foreign exchange. It's an extraordinarily beautiful island, tropical and mountainous. And if you're coming from New York, it's literally paradise!

Nearly 80 percent of Grenada's exports go to Europe, and most of its imports come from Britain, Canada, and Trinidad. It conducts very little trade with the United States. This will make it that much more difficult for U.S. imperialism to put a *direct* trade squeeze on Grenada. They will have to work through their allied imperialist governments, and this throws a spotlight on mobilizing solidarity with Grenada in Canada, Britain, and Western Europe.

Until the late 1950s, when Grenada was still under direct colonial rule, its British rulers maintained a law banning the construction of industry on the island. A little industry developed nonetheless, but the official policy was to bar it.

About one-third of Grenada's workforce are directly involved in agriculture. Since the late 1940s, however, there has been a substantial increase in the size of the urban working class, particularly in services, commerce, gas and electricity, construction, transportation, and dock workers. By the early 1970s the number of workers employed in small manufacturing had reached nearly 2,500—almost 9 percent of the employed workforce.

At the time of the revolution, the yearly per capita income in U.S. dollars was around $300, and the unemployment rate was around 50 percent.

Jobs and Development

Faced with this situation, the revolution's accomplishments in just a short sixteen months are very impressive.

Some 2,500 new jobs have been created, lowering the unemployment rate from about 50 percent to 35 percent, according to government estimates. Clearly, a 35 percent unemployment rate is still very high, posing problems not only for the people who have no jobs, but also big political and economic challenges to the revolution and its ability to move forward.

The new government recognizes that the primary solution to this problem is agricultural development, both for domestic consumption and for export. This involves not only expansion of agricultural production itself, but also the development of related industries—processing plants, canneries, and so on. Included in this is tapping the island's fishing wealth for the first time; this will be a new source of food, export earnings, and jobs.

The development of Grenada's tourism will also play an important, although lesser, role in economic growth and job creation.

In addition, there is a tremendous amount of work to be done simply building and rebuilding roads, water lines, housing, schools, and other socially useful projects.

Before the revolution, Grenada imported roughly three-quarters of its food. This is not necessary in fertile Grenada. It is a wasteful nonuse of resources. So the PRG has plans to reverse this situation.

With the development of the fishing industry and construction of refrigeration and processing plants, the government is beginning to provide fish to the population.

It also plans to meet domestic sugar needs within two years. At one time, Grenada was the second largest sugar producer in the Caribbean.

And there is diversification into other foods, once again both for domestic consumption and for export.

The government has recently launched a land reform program. This is important for three reasons: (1) jobs; (2) food production; and (3) overall economic development.

Of course, there's a fourth very important *political* reason. That is the need to forge and solidify an alliance between the urban workers and the rural toilers—small farmers and agricultural laborers.

The government already owns about one-third of all estates over 100 acres; that accounts for some 40 percent of the arable land. This is not primarily the result of nationalization since the revolution. Most were Crown lands, British lands, that were turned over to the Gairy regime when Grenada won its formal independence in 1974. At the time of the March 1979 revolution, these simply fell into the possession of the new government.

On this land, the government is establishing agricultural cooperatives and beginning the construction of agro-industrial projects. These production and marketing co-ops are administered by the government in collaboration with the Agricultural Workers Councils, which have been formed since the revolution to organize the rural poor, small peasants, and agricultural workers who work on these and other farms. In addition to the wages paid to the agricultural workers, the revenues of these state farms are divided, with one-third split among the workers on that particular farm, one-third plowed back into reinvestment, and one-third for schools, roads, and other government development projects.

The government has also established, for the first time ever in rural areas, the practice of equal pay for equal work for women. And it has gone out to these areas to explain the importance of this to the agricultural workers, since wage equality had been totally unheard-of.

There are also a few dozen large, privately owned estates on the island. A large farm on an island of this size—133 square miles—is usually something in the range of 100 acres. There are a few that are up to 500 acres.

Some 35 percent of the arable land is in the hands of small farmers who own very small plots.

Perhaps the key fact for the opening stage of the agrarian reform is that *one-third* of Grenada's arable land is not utilized at all, it is simply lying fallow. So the government has launched its reform under the slogan, "Idle land for idle hands," which ties together utilizing the unemployed labor power of Grenadians and implementing the agrarian reform.

No confiscation of private estates is projected in the initial stage. The government instead set up a commission that has been identifying idle lands for lease or sale to the government. On these lands, the government has begun establishing cooperatives, drawing workers from among the agricultural workforce, small farmers who can be attracted to join the cooperatives, and the urban jobless. Government agencies are providing financing, training, administration and extension services. These agencies also help the co-ops find markets both in Grenada and in other Caribbean islands or overseas. The cooperatives are owned and operated by the workers, who are organized by the Agricultural Workers Councils.

There's an aspect of this program that poses a particularly tough challenge; that is, attracting the urban unemployed onto the land, to farm, and to become involved in the agro-industrial projects. So the government has launched a campaign, including material incentives, to win and convince urban youth to participate. The aim is to attract growing layers of youth, as well as agricultural workers and small peasants, by showing them that these cooperatives can provide a better life and more efficient production.

Intimately tied to this, as I've said before, is the development of agro-industry. Until March 1979, most of Grenada's agricultural products were exported to Britain for processing. The nutmeg was exported and ground into nutmeg powder abroad, for example.

So, the new government is building up its own processing plants, and this is the central aspect of its current industrial development plans. A new coffee plant has already been built, as well as several nutmeg processing factories. Fish canneries, refrigeration plants, and a furniture industry are also getting under way.

Through this process, the government is already on the way to becoming the largest industrial producer and employer. And taking a page from the *Communist Manifesto,* a recent issue of the weekly *New Jewel* added that one of the things the "PRG wants to do is to help break down the artificial difference between town and country created by colonialism and Gairyism."

Social Gains

There have been big accomplishments in education, as well.

What was the situation when the New Jewel Movement came to power? About 40 percent of the population was functionally illiterate. As Bishop pointed out in the interview he gave to *IP,* after 350 years, the colonialists had only been able to construct *one* public secondary school on the entire island. The others are church-run.

Nearly 90 percent of the population have had only primary education. And in 1978, the last full year of Gairy's rule, there were only three Grenadians receiving university education. And one of them was Gairy's daughter!

Since the revolution, this situation is being turned around. There are now 109 university scholarships, 109 students receiving a university education. Secondary school fees have been lowered from $37.50 to $12.50, and the government projects free secondary education by 1981. They've instituted a free milk and cheap hot lunch program for all elementary school children. They're about to launch a literacy campaign modeled on that in Cuba and Nicaragua—organized by the Centre for Popular Education.

And the government has also set up four vocational training schools—one for fishing, one for farming, one for tourism, and one for forestry. This is in addition to the school that is conducted by Cubans at the international airport site to train Grenadians in how to operate heavy equipment and learn skilled construction trades.

The overall aim of the educational reforms is to more closely integrate work and study at all levels in the schools.

There have also been important strides in health. Not only has the number of doctors been doubled, but care is being provided virtually for free. For the first time, clinics have been established in the two small islands, Petit Martinique and Cariacou, off the main island. About 9 percent of the new 1980 budget is allotted to health.

The government has also launched a major housing reconstruction and repair program. Much of the island of Grenada itself has electrification, but most people on Petit Martinique and Carriacou will soon be receiving electricity for the first time.

Seven out of ten Grenadians did not have running water, so this is a big project now under way.

The new 1980 budget, which the Grenadians proudly call the first working-class budget in Grenada's history, is EC$103 million. Of that EC$103 million, EC$21.5 million is allotted to health and education.

EC$43 million is set for capital expenditures to help develop the economy. The biggest single item is the construction of the international airport, but this figure also includes funds for the agro-industrial projects, farms, fisheries, road reconstruction, and so on.

The budget will also lift the burden of taxation off the backs of working people. It entirely wipes off taxation for 30 percent of the workers who had previously been taxed; this includes almost all agricultural workers and industrial workers. Other workers will receive a flat 21 percent tax cut, along with increased personal, child, and school allowances.

At the same time, the government has levied a new 25 percent tax on profits going abroad, a 20 percent tax on rents going abroad, and stiffer taxes on Grenadian businessmen and landlords.

The PRG has also begun a National Commercial Bank. Before the revolution, there was no Grenadian-owned bank on the island. All banking was controlled by British capital—Barclay's—or Canadian capital.

The eventual aim of the new government is to nationalize banking and insurance, without which planned economic development and regulation is inconceivable. But such a move in the first year of the revolution—in the absence of *any* domestic banking capital—would have been disastrous for the small farmers, fishermen, cab drivers, and small businessmen who depend on credit for their livelihood. It would also have negatively affected the PRG's capacity to get international loans and aid. (For similar reasons, the Nicaraguan government nationalized all domestic banking but has so far only slapped stiff controls on foreign-owned banks.)

So, the initial move by the NJM-led government has been the launching of the National Commercial Bank, which in the first six months has amassed EC$6 million in assets. This is modest, but it has allowed the government to begin providing easy credit terms to workers, farmers, and fishermen, and developing an added source of investment capital under its control. This will facilitate further moves towards development on a planned basis.

The NJM's 1973 manifesto presented its initial thinking on this: "We believe that no country can be independent unless it owns and controls the banks and the insurance companies," it said. " . . . Our plan is to nationalise the banks at the earliest correct opportunity and to use the money to finance directly the new agricultural and agro-industrial schemes, as well as our new plans for tourism and fisheries . . . we condemn foreign ownership of our banks."

A related problem facing Grenada is that it has no currency of its own. Along with several other former British colonies, it uses the East Caribbean Currency, so the monetary authority is not under its control. Along with the obvious economic problems posed by this situation, it also leaves the PRG politically vulnerable, as we saw in the early days of the revolution, when the body that administers the ECC delayed currency shipments for a period as a warning to the new government.

The PRG has also established a National Importing Board. Through import controls, prices on rice, sugar, and cement have been brought down by 10 to 20 percent.

Mass Organizations

By far the most important conquest of the Grenada revolution has been the construction and extension of the mass organizations and mass participation in the revolutionary process. This is the view of the NJM leadership, as well. The government actively fosters the organization and mobilization of the workers and farmers and seeks every opportunity to help raise their class consciousness.

Unionization on the island has gone up from 30 percent under Gairy to 85 percent just in the past sixteen months. The PRG has wiped all antilabor legislation off the books, and the government has frequently intervened on the side of the workers in labor-management disputes—around sexual harassment of women, firings, or other antilabor practices.

A New Jewel Women's Organization has been established. And there have already been important advances for women—equal pay for equal work, a new maternity benefits law, greater access to education.

The militias were launched in the early days of the revolution, but they have been growing especially fast only since the June 19 counterrevolutionary terror bombing. The government has now projected a militia of 20,000—about a fifth of the island's population.

The New Jewel Movement is also building a National Youth Organization across the island. Young people are also involved in the National Students' Council and in Youth for Reconstruction, which draws young people into useful reconstruction projects and helps to alleviate the effects of unemployment.

In each of the six parishes, there are parish committees of the NJM and its supporters. These committees call together periodic mass meetings where NJM and PRG leaders present government proposals, hear discussion and debate, and get feedback for the process of policy-making by the new government.

As yet, there is no formal structure to these popular committees, such as that being developed in Cuba through the People's Power Assemblies. The NJM plans to move in this direction, but the pace and forms are still undecided. Whatever the outcome of these deliberations, the NJM and PRG have clearly demonstrated their desire to promote mass involvement in charting Grenada's future.

Workers and Farmers Government

This brings us to the central question we need to discuss: the recognition of the evidence that this government, as shown by its *actions*, is a workers and farmers government with a revolutionary proletarian leadership, a Marxist leadership.

The NJM-led government has displaced the political power of the Grenadian capitalists, both the Gairyites and the anti-Gairy bourgeois opposition. It has stood up to the imperialists. It has taken decisive action against the counterrevolution. It has carried out measures in the interests of the workers and farmers and against the interests of their exploiters.

These are the actions of what our Transitional Program calls "a government independent of the bourgeoisie," or what was described in the "Theses on Tactics" at the Fourth Congress of the Communist International as a government "born out of struggle of the masses, supported by workers' bodies which are capable of fighting, bodies created by the most oppressed sections of the working masses."

The PRG has its origins in the fight against a semicolonial capitalist dictatorship. It was brought to power at the head of an anti-imperialist movement that developed an explicitly socialist leadership. Revolutionary Cuba is the acknowledged model for the kind of society the PRG is seeking to build in Grenada.

The New Jewel Movement came to power through an insurrection. Its call for mass support to that uprising was successful because of the NJM's previous record of struggle and its growing links with the workers in the cities and in the countryside.

The new government has repeatedly demonstrated its resoluteness in standing up to imperialism and combating the counterrevolution. The old state apparatus has been destroyed. The new government has constructed a new state apparatus from the ground up. Gairy's old army and police have been dismantled, as has his extralegal terror squad, the Mongoose Gang. A new People's Revolutionary Army and Grenada Police Service have been built, as well as a militia. All these are led by the NJM and its supporters, and are based on working-class and rural youth.

There is a twenty-three person government and, drawn from it, a smaller cabinet. Only the cabinet is involved in day-to-day governmental tasks. All the decisive posts in this government are held by NJM cadres. There are only four capitalists in the government, and only one of them is in the cabinet—Norris Bain, minister of health and housing.

The government administration under Gairy was so corrupt and rotten that it has been thoroughly cleaned out and replaced. This has meant a big challenge for the revolution, since many young, inexperienced militants have been brought in to conduct a wide variety of governmental tasks. It is a big job trying to figure out how to reorganize things, put them back together, and begin to move forward. It reminds you of late 1959 and 1960 in Cuba—young fighters working long and hard to build a new government.

These new structures, the revolutionary direction of the government, its consistent measures responding to the class interests of the Grenadian workers and farmers, and *against* the interests of imperialism and the domestic exploiters—these are decisive evidence for us.

There is another part of the Theses on Tactics from the Fourth Comintern Congress that we often point to.

"The overriding tasks of the workers' government," it says, "must be to arm the proletariat, to disarm the bourgeois, counterrevolutionary organizations, to introduce the control of production, to transfer the main burden of taxation to the rich, and to break the resistance of the counterrevolutionary bourgeoisie."

This is a good summary of what the NJM has set out to do and is accomplishing.

In past party documents—such as the July 1960 article by Joe Hansen on the Cuban workers and farmers government—we have referred to the capacity of such governments "to undertake measures against the bourgeois political power and bourgeois property relations."

"The extent of these measures is not decisive in determining the nature of the regime," Joe said. "What is decisive is the capacity and the tendency" of the government to move along this road.

As we've seen, this new Grenadian government has shown its capacity to take decisive measures against bourgeois *political* power. And it has already taken major steps to limit and control the economic power of the remaining capitalists.

But because of the extreme dependence and underdevelopment of Grenada's economy, and the early stage in mobilizing and educating the workers to control and manage the economy, the PRG has correctly not yet carried out substantial expropriations of capitalist property.

The New Jewel Movement leadership understands that the PRG will have to expropriate the imperialist-owned banks and insurance companies; the major privately owned industries and commercial establishments; the big estates; and the imperialist-owned and large local tourist hotels. The NJM makes no secret of this; most of these measures are outlined in its 1973 manifesto.

Without such measures, the government cannot implement thorough planning to develop the economy and raise the living standards of the masses. Moreover, the laws of capital accumulation will press toward strengthening the economic position of the exploiters. This will be true, even though the PRG is developing a larger and larger government-owned sector through the establishment of agro-industries, fishing, and so on.

But today, the new government is still not ready to undertake major nationalizations. It still needs the skills and techniques it can't yet replace. It needs jobs to help alleviate unemployment, and the government itself is not yet creating enough jobs through its own development projects.

Most of all, the new revolutionary government needs the time to organize, educate, and prepare the workers and toilers to exercise control over production, to run the economy, and to begin to govern.

Of course, this is the fundamental social contradiction that—to a greater or lesser extent in different situations—faces a workers and farmers government. The government is based on the class interests of the toilers, while it still must defend the preservation of capitalist property relations in substantial sectors of the economy.

Like all contradictions, this one has never been, and cannot be, resolved harmoniously. Of course, from the standpoint of the toilers, it is advantageous for as harmonious a transition as possible—one that involves the least disruption of production, dislocation of social life, and destruction of life and property.

But such matters are resolved not by wishes or intentions, but by the conflict of classes and the caliber of their leaderships, as well as the world relationship of class forces at the given time. Many factors can force confrontations and expropriations well before economic criteria alone would dictate: capitalist sabotage of production, decapitalization, refusal to abide by legislation to protect workers' interests, imperialist pressure, counterrevolutionary plots.

In addition, the workers and farmers themselves take initiatives. Sometimes these may be premature, but often they respond to and counter dangers as yet unnoticed by the leadership, propelling the entire revolutionary process forward.

This conflict between exploiters and exploited, and interplay between the toilers and the leaders of the revolution, provides the framework in which the social contradictions are resolved in life; the concrete manifestations vary widely in different countries and situations.

These are the kinds of questions that Mary-Alice [Waters] dealt with in her presentation to the conference last Sunday—the experiences and problems that Lenin, Trotsky, and the rest of the Bolsheviks had to grapple with, the same kinds of questions the Sandinistas face today in Nicaragua.

Revolutionary Proletarian Leadership

Back in 1960, when Joe wrote about the workers and farmers government in Cuba, he had this to say about the political development of the Castro leadership at that time:

"Enjoying the support of the workers and peasants, having led them in a political revolution, faced with the imperative need to carry the revolution forward to its culmination by toppling bourgeois economic and social relations and extending the revolution throughout Latin America and into the United States, the regime lacks the socialist consciousness (program) to accomplish this. Even if it carries out extensive expropriations, these, precisely because of this lack of socialist consciousness, are not so assured as to be considered a permanent foundation of the state. In its bourgeois consciousness, the regime falls short of the objective needs of the revolution."

Of course, this is one of the things that has changed, that is so different and so important about this political current that we see developing and moving forward in the Caribbean and Central America. Because of the Marxist development of the Cuban leadership, and because of the example that has been set by the socialist revolution in Cuba, the New Jewel Movement, like the FSLN, *does* start out with socialist consciousness. It *does* have a program and a perspective to lead the process forward, as well as the experiences of twenty years of Cuba to learn from. And its basic strategy and perspectives do not fall short of the objective needs of the Grenada revolution.

This is our assessment of the revolutionary capacities that have been exhibited by this leadership. They are Marxist leaders of the working class. That is what we've seen in the FSLN, what we've seen in the NJM, and what we hope to collaborate with and see more of coming out of the rise in the Central American and Caribbean revolution.

The NJM leaders, like us, recognize the antagonism between the class character of their government and the continuing existence of substantial bourgeois economic power. The NJM knows from its own experience what the existence of that bourgeois economic power can mean for helping the capitalists politically hold on to points of support, and, more importantly, for undermining the revolution at its base, through their ability to sabotage production, disrupt planning, and in that way to demoralize, confuse, and demobilize the working masses.

The NJM not only recognizes this contradiction, they deal with it. They are faced daily with it in life. And they are resolving it by organizing the Grenadian workers and peasants to push forward along the line of march leading toward a socialist Grenada.

Let's look for a few minutes at how the NJM itself explains the character and current stage of the Grenada revolution.

The NJM's slogan is "Let those who labor hold the reins." I think that's an accurate, although condensed, expression of what they're attempting to accomplish and how they have proceeded.

In the early days of the revolution, Prime Minister Bishop said that "in the current stage, what we have is a national democratic revolution in Grenada." This is a scientifically correct description of the key initial tasks that have faced this revolution: getting rid of the dictatorship; lifting the burden of imperialist political domination and beginning to strike at the roots of imperialist economic domination; the expansion of democratic rights; beginning to deal with the agrarian question and food production; restarting the economy; ensuring decent conditions for workers and wiping antilabor statutes off the books.

Another long-time New Jewel Movement leader, Finance Minister Bernard Coard, said at about the same time that, "Our primary objective at this point in time is not building socialism, quite frankly, but simply trying to get the economy, which has been totally shattered by Gairy, back on its feet."

The NJM leaders believe that only a workers government can accomplish these things. They use many different terms—people's government, people's democratic government, workers government, workers and farmers government. But the content of all of them is clear.

In Ernie's interview with Selwyn Strachan last October, here's what this top NJM leader had to say:

". . . we call ourselves socialists. . . . We see the workers as the revolutionary class in society, and we are determined to raise their political and ideological consciousness. We say we are a workers government, and we are determined to improve the quality of life of the worker."

Strachan went on to explain that the NJM and PRG "devote a lot of time to the building of the political and class consciousness of the workers in our society."

Those of you who've read the speeches by New Jewel Movement and union leader Vincent Noel in *IP* or the *Militant* can confirm that these comrades are dead serious about trying to build the political and class consciousness of Grenadian workers. Noel gave the speech at the end of a union-sponsored seminar for worker cadres. I want to read a little bit of what he had to say, because it was one of the best short, popular explanations of *our* political approach to the trade unions that I have ever heard.

"There are some who tell us that the trade unions should have nothing to do with whether or not we have full employment," he said, or "what the cost of living is, whether or not we have education, whether or not we have health services, whether or not we have corruption in government, whether we have brutality, and all the other ills. There are some who tell you that this is not the trade unions' business.

"What we are saying here is that *every single thing* that affects the society is the workers' business, because workers form the majority of the society, and in fact they support the entire society through their labor. . . .

"Comrades, brothers and sisters," Noel continued, "we face a difficult period in our history. We have to decide for ourselves what our future will be. And there's no other appropriate group to decide what the future will be than, of course, the working class. Because we are the ones who are working; we are the ones who are producing; we are the ones who are keeping the economy afloat, keeping the country afloat.

"And therefore in what is done, we have to play a leading role in guiding and shaping it. We have to make sure that what is done is always in our interests."

This is how the NJM leadership is educating the workers of Grenada. Not just in speeches and seminars, but in articles in the *New Jewel* and the *Free West Indian*, on billboards along the roads, and what you hear over Radio Free Grenada.

They also try to teach the workers about solidarity, and about their responsibility to take the leadership of all the oppressed of Grenadian society.

"We are trying to ally the other classes in society with the workers," Selwyn Strachan told Ernie. "In other words, we see the struggle in a wider context. Not just as a working-class struggle on behalf of workers, but linking that, trying to bring all the oppressed classes into alliance with the working class to fight for all the democratic, progressive measures at this particular stage in the struggle.

"The peasantry," Strachan said, "is the single largest category of people in the country. It is twice as strong as the working class, maybe one-and-a-half times stronger. And then we have all these other people around, the artisans, the fishermen, the small and medium sized businessmen, and so forth."

The Grenadians are seeking to achieve what the Bolsheviks taught. Under a workers and farmers government, the trade unions must become schools for socialism, schools for the workers to learn to manage the economy, lead the entire country, and govern.

Capitalist Stage of Development

Does the New Jewel Movement see the need for a capitalist stage of development? Does it see a need for a governmental alliance with the capitalist class? Does it see a role for any section of the capitalist class in leading the revolutionary process forward?

The answer in each case is, "no."

When our French comrade, Alain Krivine, was down in Grenada, he conducted an interview with another NJM leader, George Louison.

"We've never hidden that we are struggling for socialism. This is in our program and we consider our party to be a vanguard socialist party," Louison told Krivine. "Our relations with bourgeois parties are nonexistent. In the past when we entered an alliance with them, for instance against facism [Gairyism], we always preserved our independence as a party."

Then Louison went on to say that while there are a few "businessmen in the government, politically men of the left-center," they "are no obstacle to the revolutionary measures." This has been shown to be true by the actual course of the PRG.

In his interview with Ernie, Strachan laid out very clearly the dynamic of this revolution—a dynamic strikingly similar to what the Bolsheviks were trying to accomplish in the months after October 1917. The NJM is committed not to bring war communism down on itself, if that can be avoided.

The NJM, in practice, is leading the Grenadian workers and farmers along the path of the permanent revolution. Not the Stalinist caricature of permanent revolution, nor the ultraleft sectarian caricature of permanent revolution—which is the theory Prime Minister Bishop aptly labelled the "instant coffee" theory of revolution.

Such caricatures have nothing to do with permanent revolution. Permanent revolution actually explains how the revolution: 1) cannot take place under the leadership of any wing of the bourgeoisie, but must take place under the leadership of the working class allied with the poor peasants; 2) immediately tackles the national, democratic, agrarian, and anti-imperialist tasks, as well as measures ensuring labor rights, improving the conditions of the workers, and expanding their control at the expense of the capitalists; and 3) grows over as a *permanent* process, pushing these tasks to the limit, to the uniquely socialist tasks of expropriating the bourgeoisie and establishing a planned economy.

Strachan laid out for Ernie a detailed explanation of how the NJM sees the development of the Grenada revolution:

> We feel that whilst we move rapidly to raise the consciousness of the working people, including the working class, at the same time we have to consolidate our position in certain sectors of the economy, which will again help to strengthen our position, raising the level of the productive forces.
>
> In other words, we see us moving toward socialism, using the mixed-economy approach, the noncapitalist path at this stage. And that, of course, will help us increase the strength of the working class in our country, prepare us for the advancement to socialism, where we can eventually have the dictatorship of the proletariat.
>
> But now it is impossible. We have to keep up the political education work. We have to do work among the workers, work among the farmers, work among the fishermen, work among the women, the youth, and even the small and medium sized businesspeople, the middle strata, and unite the population and prepare them for the next stage of the struggle.
>
> In other words, we see this as a democratic phase of the struggle, preparing the masses for the transition to socialism.

Of course, taken in isolation from what the NJM and PRG are actually doing, some of the terminology used by Strachan—"mixed economy" and "noncapitalist path"—has been and is still used by bourgeois nationalist figures such as Nasser, Nyerere, and reformist Communist parties to chart a course away from the socialist revolution, a course that is not "noncapitalist" at all.

The content given these terms by the actual practice of the NJM leadership, however, is the opposite. When they speak of a "mixed economy approach," they are stating an indisputable fact about their economy right now and making the correct point that changing this will be a process, as Strachan put it, of "preparing the masses for the transition."

What they mean by the "noncapitalist path" was made clear by Strachan's answer to Ernie's next question.

"Do you see this [process] in terms of distinct historical stages?" Ernie asked.

He had in mind the Stalinist conception whereby an allegedly progressive wing of the national bourgeoisie plays a leading role in the initial stage of the revolution. According to this schema, this gives rise to a "noncapitalist" road that is, so to speak, neither Paraguay nor Cuba.

A third way—exemplified by Nkrumah's Ghana or Nyerere's Tanzania, for example.

The Stalinists use this "theory" as cover for subordinating the workers to the capitalists in order to head off revolutions. And where revolutions do occur, to head off their development in the direction charted twenty years ago by the Castro leadership. This, for example, is the policy and practice of reformist Communist parties throughout Latin America.

Strachan's answer to Ernie makes it crystal clear that the NJM totally rejects any such idea.

"This, as we see it, is a distinct historical stage," Strachan said.

> It is the democratic process. And in the democratic process, one has to look at all these factors.
>
> The aim, of course, is socialism. But socialism cannot just come, just so. We have to prepare the ground for that social transformation. We see it now as democratizing the society, making sure that all the rights of the working people are fully entrenched, making sure that the economy is consolidated, having a full grip on the key sectors of the economy, and increasing the overall level of productive forces, which will prepare us for the transition.
>
> In other words, we are moving to socialism, bypassing capitalist development.

Finally, the clearest indication of the NJM's course is its explicit identification with the Cuban revolution, its attempt to learn and incorporate the lessons from that revolution and the Castro leadership, and its record of doing just that.

Strachan told Ernie that he believed Grenada's "course of development will be more or less the same as the Cuban revolution. There may be one or two minor differences, but nothing dramatic."

There are two important differences, however.

First, from the very outset in Grenada, full political power has been consolidated in the hands of a pro-working class leadership. That's one of the lessons the Grenadians were able to draw from the Cubans, who had to contend with recalcitrant bourgeois forces in the government during the first six months of their revolution.

Second, the Grenada revolution takes place at a time when the Cuban revolution has been a living revolution for twenty years, with its example of internationalism and social development. The Grenada revolution occurs at a much more favorable stage in the development of the world class struggle. This fact makes a revolution even in a small country like Grenada a very important and hopeful event.

"The more Cuban-type governments, the better for us," Strachan told Ernie. "But of course, Cuba's the only one yet."

Although we can add—Not for long.

This points to another way in which the NJM leadership is charting a way forward along the road of permanent revolution. That is, their profound conviction, which they act on and proclaim to the entire world, that the defense and progress of the socialist revolution in any country is inseparably linked to the *extension* of the socialist revolution to other countries.

The NJM leaders recognize that the task of constructing a workers state in Grenada necessitates raising the class consciousness, mobilization, and participation of the workers and peasants.

When Comrade Liam James spoke at the Caribbean solidarity rally the other night, he explained that taking power was only a small part of the job. How to actually lead the revolution forward is the big challenge, he said.

When Andrew, Diane, and I were down in Grenada, we were granted an interview for *IP* with Bishop. We asked what he saw as the main political characteristics of the revolution. [See Appendix II for complete interview.]

He told us that there are three main pillars.

First, he said, is the "organization and mobilization of the masses. That is very key. To always try to fully involve the masses in whatever we are trying to do, to keep them fully involved, to ensure that they understand what the problems are and where we are trying to go."

Second, he said, is the question of national security and defense.

And third, "building a sound national economy and bringing more benefits to the people, improving the quality of their lives."

This leadership understands that there are no bureaucratic shortcuts, no alternatives to involvement of the masses, and to deepening the revolution through strengthening the mass organizations, and using the power of the government to push this process forward.

Bishop told us that "all three [of these pillars] have to be worked on at the same time. We cannot afford to let any drop or lag behind"—neither the mass organization, nor the social measures, nor the national defense.

If you don't progress on all three fronts, the revolution will be in trouble.

Some Examples

I want to give a few examples of how this leadership relies on the power and consciousness of the workers to advance the revolution.

First, let's look at how the PRG went about developing a maternity benefits law. Government leaders didn't simply decree the law. They circulated a draft of it to the unions, to the women's organizations, to the parish committees, and to other organizations for discussion, for suggestions to improve the bill. Most places they got some good ideas and general agreement.

But in the discussion in the Grenada Trade Union Council, the representatives of the teachers union opposed the law. Of course, given the overwhelming majority support elsewhere in Grenada, the new government would have been within its rights to go ahead and decree the maternity benefits law to cover all women workers. But it said, "Okay, the law will cover almost all workers, but initially it will not apply to teachers."

Then, the New Jewel Movement launched a political campaign inside the teachers union against the leadership's backward position. At the next union election, an NJM-led slate won the leadership. It demanded maternity benefits for the members, and the PRG responded by extending the maternity benefits law to cover women teachers. In the process, a whole layer of workers in the teachers union who had been miseducated by their previous misleaders had their class consciousness raised.

This is also how the PRG approached the question of equal pay for equal work for women. In some rural areas this was a very new idea and was not initially understood as an advance. So Prime Minister Bishop and other NJM and PRG leaders went out and held meetings with workers to explain why women agricultural workers should receive the same pay for equal work as male agricultural workers.

A second example is how the leadership responded to the June 19 counterrevolutionary terror bombing at a large rally in St. George's. The attempt to kill the central leaders of the revolution failed, but three young women were murdered and dozens injured in the explosion. Rather than allowing this to demobilize, discourage, and frighten the masses—which it had the potential to do—Bishop went on Radio Free Grenada that same night and gave a major address to the nation.

He pointed to the horror of the cold-blooded maimings and murders as an example of what counterrevolution and imperialism will stoop to. He explained that the enemies of the revolution will undertake further efforts to prevent the workers and farmers from controlling their country and improving their lives. The experience was turned into another launching pad from which to strengthen the mass organizations and begin a drive, which has already been very successful, to expand the militia. Thousands of workers for the first time felt they, concretely, and individually, had a reason to join the militia.

The third example is how the new government dealt with the *Torchlight*, the main capitalist weekly newspaper. In the early days of the revolution, the *Torchlight* used its resources and facilities to spread lies and slanders about the NJM all around the island. It became a focal point for all those who sought to undermine the revolution. It went so far as to carry close-up photographs of Bishop's bodyguards and a front-page photograph of a People's Revolutionary Army camp that was under construction, along with its location.

Last October, supporters of the revolution held a series of demonstrations against *Torchlight* outside its offices.

That same month, a rightist plot was uncovered, a plot by leaders of the two main bourgeois parties, the GNP and UPP. The government discovered arms, ammunition, maps, and plans for a coup attempt. At this point, the government temporarily shut down the *Torchlight*.

Following the shutdown, the PRG and NJM stepped up their efforts—which they had been conducting all along in response to the paper's slanders—to explain what freedom of the press really amounts to under capitalism. That it was freedom of the buck, freedom of the dollar. For example, they exposed the fact that the *Trinidad Express*, a reactionary newspaper in Trinidad, and a big Grenadian capitalist by the name of D.M.B. Cromwell each owned more than 4,500 shares in the *Torchlight* and thereby controlled what it said.

Then, the PRG passed the Democratic Newspaper Law, which barred foreigners from owning shares in Grenadian newspapers and stipulated that no Grenadian could own more than 4 percent of the shares of any newspaper. This having been done, the *New Jewel* ran an article with the headline, "Stop holding up *Torchlight!*" It pointed out that Cromwell and *Trinidad Express* "have now decided that they will not reopen the Torchlight newspaper. They are saying that the P.R.G. must repeal the Democratic Newspaper Law or they will not start to print again."

The *New Jewel* went on to explain what the new law said. "These measures are to ensure that the newspaper becomes more national and that it reflects the *true* development of the Grenada Revolution. Every Grenadian working person will then have the chance to express their views instead of them just being thrown into the waste paper baskets."

Referring to Cromwell and the *Trinidad Express*, the

article said that, "N.J.M. calls on these enemies of Democracy to stop *holding back* the opening of the Torchlight. *Let genuine freedom of the press flow in this country.* No one man, or two men, must hold back the freedom of the Press."

And they're still waiting for Cromwell and the *Trinidad Express* to meet their challenge. By handling the matter in this way, the class consciousness of the whole population was raised, and the attempt by the *Torchlight* and the imperialists to whip up a campaign in Grenada about freedom of the press was effectively undercut.

The government has taken a similar approach to opponents of the revolution within the church. Counterrevolutionaries in the Catholic church hierarchy both inside and outside Grenada, began through various methods to undermine the revolution and spread lies and rumors.

So Prime Minister Bishop answered with a major speech. He stressed the new government's "fullest commitment to freedom of worship and religion." He urged "cooperation with the churches in all areas that will bring social and material benefits to our people." And he pledged not "to tell the church how to conduct its religious activities."

"But by the same token," Bishop said, "we are not prepared to allow the church or elements within the church to . . . use their influence and standing as religious leaders to engage in counterrevolutionary activities against the interests of the people."

In this way, the NJM has divided the church, more and more isolating those consciously bourgeois elements who hope to use it as a weapon against the revolution. Jerry Hunnicutt told me that at the International Women's Day Rally this year, one of the speakers was from the Young Women's Christian Association. She ended her speech with a clenched fist and the slogan "God bless our revolution!"

Ganja, Cars, and Houses

One of the most politically important examples is how the PRG and NJM went about countering the marijuana growers—"*ganja*" growers, as they are called in Grenada. The ganja growers were attempting to open up big tracts of land to marijuana cultivation—which is more profitable than nutmeg or food products. At the same time, they sought to use this issue to mobilize young people, and even some agricultural workers, against the revolution. So the ganja growers held a demonstration when the new government moved to return lands taken over for marijuana cultivation.

The New Jewel Movement responded by organizing several large counterdemonstrations of workers, farmers, and youth. And the May 17 issue of the *New Jewel* ran an article explaining why these marches had been called.

"Some of our people are asking why don't we just pick up the Ganja leaders instead of organizing marches against them," the *New Jewel* said. "We say that *anytime imperialism organizes counterrevolutionaries against the Revolution the people must answer them by showing the strength of the Revolution.*

"The strength of the Grenada Revolution lies in its popularity among the people, not only in the strength of the armed forces."

Then the article cited the negative example of Chile. One of the big problems in Chile, it said, was that when the CIA-backed rightists began to mobilize, they were not answered by mass working-class and peasant mobilizations. "This was one of the most important things leading to the fall of the Allende Government," it said.

"If the people just sit by and allow the counterrevolutionaries to organize, and *we* do not organize, *their* strength will increase while ours decreases. If we allowed them to be in political control of the streets, it would appear as though the people are weak and it would encourage other opportunists and criminal elements to join them. We must *demonstrate* our strength as the majority. . . . That is why we march. Our people are our Revolution."

This is exactly how the Castro leadership in Cuba responds to imperialist attacks, as it has done with marches of up to 5 million people over the past several months. It is the way the Sandinistas are answering those, inside and outside Nicaragua, who try to sabotage the advance of the revolution.

How different from the methods of the Stalinists! How different from the bureaucratic, petty bourgeois methods of the People's Democratic Party of Afghanistan; which did such damage to revolutionary prospects in that country.

The leaderships in Cuba, Grenada, and Nicaragua are determined to show the worker and peasant majority that *it* has the power to fight for its class interests and combat its class enemies. These are leaderships that teach the toilers that their strength lies in looking to their own battalions and those of the oppressed and exploited around the world—*not* to the government apparatus, *not* to some allegedly progressive wing of the capitalist ruling classes.

Just on final example. How have the PRG and NJM begun to deal with the question of bureaucratism and privilege?

For one thing, when the NJM came to power, it slashed all ministerial salaries by one-third.

But a more revealing example is how the NJM handled the case of Ralph Thompson. He was a member of the New Jewel Movement who, after the revolution, got the idea that he should be given a free house and car. This runs entirely counter to PRG policy. No one in the government is given a car unless they specifically need it for their work—employees of the agricultural extension services, for example. Bishop, the prime minister, still uses his own small car, which he owned before the revolution.

So when the government refused to give Thompson a car or house, he launched a little campaign around the issue. The NJM answered through an editorial in the *New Jewel*.

The editorial did not have even a trace of any attempts to slander Thompson or repudiate and discredit his past record—a crude method so common to the Stalinists when they break, for any reason, with a past member or leader.

"This Comrade was a member of the Party and a strong fighter against Gairy," the *New Jewel* said. "He worked tirelessly selling the newspaper and beating back Gairy's propaganda. His contribution to the struggle cannot be denied.

"But Ralph Thompson believes that Party members have a right to receive 'special favours'."

Unable to convince Thompson, the NJM had to suspend him from the party, the editorial explained.

"The P.R.G. and N.J.M. say: *there will be no return to corruption in Grenada!* Benefits will reach *all* our people in time, but now, they will be distributed on the basis of who needs them most. And free 'favours' will not be given out—

to Party members, least of all, for they must stand as an example to the rest of the society."

Grenada's Internationalism

Finally, it's hard to exaggerate the internationalism of the New Jewel Movement or its importance. Especially if you heard Comrade Liam James when he spoke at the Caribbean solidarity rally last Sunday.

It infuses everything the leaders of the New Jewel Movement say and do. Upon first coming to power, this small, poor government gave $25 thousand to Zimbabwe's Patriotic Front. When the PRG approached the U.S. government for aid and were offered a paltry $5 thousand, the NJM leaders demonstratively refused to accept it and *gave* $5 thousand to Nicaragua instead. They have had African liberation solidarity rallies and expressed their solidarity with other anti-imperialist struggles around the world.

The NJM sees itself as part of a common revolutionary Marxist current along with the Cubans and Nicaraguans. Bishop explained that in the *IP* interview. The imperialists have three "concentric circles" of concern, he said.

"Into their first circle, they have certainly put Cuba, Nicaragua and Grenada as being the key countries to get at.

"Cuba for obvious reasons. It is obviously the vanguard in this region." We agree with Bishop on that point.

"Nicaragua because of its *tremendous* importance for Central America." Everybody there wants to be a Sandinista, he said.

"Grenada because of our powerful potential example for the English-speaking Caribbean countries, and indeed for the French- and Dutch-speaking Caribbean countries."

The second and third circles included countries like Jamaica, Guyana, St. Lucia, Surinam, and El Salvador where either the governments are in conflict with imperialism or where anti-imperialist struggles are making significant headway.

This is the same point that Fidel was making in his July 26 speech when he said that Grenada, Cuba, and Nicaragua are the three nations that "have shaken the yoke of imperialism in the last twenty years in a radical way, once and for all, and it is a historical imperative that one day we'll all be free. . . . all the peoples of Latin America and the Caribbean."

Bishop expressed the NJM's internationalism in other ways in the *IP* interview, as well. He said that NJM considers it "our internationalist duty" to support revolutionary fighters abroad, because, "We see the struggle as being *one* struggle, indivisible."

He solidarized with Iran, the Palestinians, Puerto Rican independence fighters, the Polisario Front in Western Sahara.

And, very important for us in the United States, Bishop expressed the NJM's confidence in "the activity, the potential, and the possiblities for the American working-class movement. Both in terms of mobilizing and organizing to stop any draft movement, and in terms of the potential of doing mortal damage to the international capitalist and imperialist system from within the belly of the main imperialist power on earth."

Moreover, this is a confidence born of substantial contact with the class struggle in the United States—as well as in Canada and Britain. Many Grenadians have either lived or frequently visited these three countries.

The NJM leaders are acquainted with *IP* and the *Militant,* as well as with the SWP and some of our activities—our record as defenders of the Cuban revolution, of Malcolm X, as champions of the struggles of the oppressed around the world, and as *participants* and *leaders* in struggles here in this country.

This acquaintance, too, was clear from the Bishop interview.

So this NJM leadership is internationalist to the core, just like the Cuban leadership and the Sandinistas.

I think that if we draw all this evidence together, there's no other conclusion to draw than that there is a workers and farmers government in Grenada, and one with a revolutionary proletarian leadership. And we want to do everything we can to collaborate with this leadership, as we do with the entire current of which it is part. We consider these comrades a sister movement and pledge ourselves to do everything possible to learn from them, collaborate with them, and defend them against imperialism.

Because the emergence of the New Jewel Movement, the emergence of the FSLN, and the extension of the revolutionary current exemplified by the Cuban revolution and the Castro leadership is important not only to the revolution in Central America and the Caribbean, but to the socialist revolution in North America and throughout the world.

SUMMARY

Let me start with two small points.

Someone passed a note asking how many people were killed during the March 13, 1979, insurrection? Just one. A commander in Gairy's army.

The second point deals with how to pronounce the name of the country. It's Grenada—with a long a, as in lemonade. If we're going to build solidarity with it, we should learn how to pronounce it.

There were some very useful contributions last night and this morning that gave us all a better feel of what's happening in the rest of the Caribbean region—the report by comrade Gilbert, a leader of the GRS of Guadeloupe and Martinique; by Richard [Fawkes], the YSA organizer in New York; Ernie [Harsch]'s information on Guyana, Trinidad and Surinam; Jerry [Hunnicutt]'s description of his observations and his discussions in Grenada five months ago; the information that Claudio [Tavarez] from the Dominican Republic and other comrades gave about the way the imperialists have divided the various Caribbean islands along language lines, and how events in Grenada can help overcome this.

These are questions we will want to follow up, so we can begin to cover political developments in the Caribbean more fully.

I want to deal primarily with the question that is at the heart of this discussion: our recognition of the New Jewel Movement as a revolutionary proletarian leadership. This conclusion is not based on any *a priori* considerations, but on observing its *actions*, the *class terms* it uses to explain its actions, and its orientation towards extending the revolution.

In this report we've been dealing specifically with the New Jewel Movement, but the overall considerations also apply to the Sandinistas and Fidelistas. In fact, the Cuban leadership, as Bishop said in the *IP* interview, is definitely in the vanguard—not simply because it has twenty years of experience, but because of the political lessons it has drawn over this period and that it has fraternally helped to generalize for other forces in Latin America and the Caribbean. We're seeing this learning process, a very important and promising process, in El Salvador and Guatemala today, as well.

During the discussion, a couple of British comrades said that they could not agree with our characterization of these leaderships—They would agree they are revolutionary, but not Marxist.

We have no desire to make a fetish out of a label. And I think we can make progress and have a productive discussion in the Fourth International short of quick agreement on a particular term.

But the underlying political question can't be avoided. It is connected to the most important responsibility and opportunity we face. It will keep posing itself again and again, as it has in our discussion in the SWP. As you begin to probe into the facts more deeply, as you study what this current does, as you read what it actually says, as you get a better understanding of its political development, the question is simply there. It makes no sense not to come to grips with it. Not to do so merely hints at narrow organizational and political sectarianism that would be deadly for our movement.

How did our discussion progress in the SWP on the Castro leadership? We started out by investigating the facts and in light of them flatly rejecting any idea that this is a reformist current or a Stalinist current. Then the question was raised by some comrades: is it perhaps a centrist current? So we discussed some of the defining characteristics of centrism—vacillation, instability, the tendency to be all talk and no action, what Trotsky eloquently captured in the phrase, "a knife without a blade." Well, that wasn't Castroism.

So these were revolutionists of some kind, we said—*revolutionists of action* is the term we settled on for a while. It seemed like a neat, accurate answer at first, but it posed a number of other obvious questions.

Does this mean they're good when it comes to action, but they have no sound ideas?

Don't *we* always strive to be revolutionists of action, too? To put our program, strategy, and tactics into practice?

How long could such a phenomenon withstand erosion? Were we saying that somehow for twenty-one years the Cubans kept stumbling onto the right path? Is it believable that despite twenty-one years of imperialist military pressure and blockade, despite twenty-one years of heavy economic and military reliance on aid from the Soviet bureaucracy, the Cubans, on the basis of enthusiasm and good intentions, empirically retained their revolutionary bearings, fought bureaucratism, and developed their internationalism to the point where they are now having a big political impact on the world balance of class forces?

How could this explain the Cuban role in and response to the extension of the *socialist* revolution to Grenada and Nicaragua? How could it explain the mobilization of 5 million Cubans last May in the face of imperialist threats? How could it explain the revolutionary example and leadership being provided by the Cubans to currents throughout the Caribbean and Central America? These were clearly something more than simply revolutionists of action who have no good ideas, who don't know how to lead and organize the working class and its allies, who don't have some profound insights into the conflict of classes on a world scale. This, after all, is a leadership that is consciously *extending the revolution.* And as Barry [Sheppard] pointed out in the discussion, that's the key dividing line between Leninism and the Stalinist counterrevolution against it.

Well, okay, you could say, they *are* trying to extend the revolution, but they are limited to anti-imperialist consciousness. They're simply trying to extend the anti-imperialist revolution. But this doesn't get you very far, either.

This current is profoundly anti-imperialist, all right. And so are we.

This current has proven in Latin America, Angola, Ethiopia, the Mideast, and Indochina that it will unconditionally stand shoulder to shoulder with any oppressed peoples fighting imperialism. That it will aid the victims of imperialist oppression however it can. That's our attitude, too.

But this certainly doesn't mean that this current is somehow limited to a narrow "anti-imperialist consciousness." That simply doesn't jibe with the facts. It can't explain what is happening in Nicaragua, in Grenada, in El Salvador.

It doesn't explain what these leaderships say or what they are *doing.* Because what all of them are putting in action is the extension, as part of the anti-imperialist, anti-dictatorial upsurges, of the socialist revolution in this hemisphere. That is what we see in Nicaragua. This is what is happening in Grenada.

In his July 26 speech, Fidel posed the question this way to the more than 100,000 Cubans gathered for the celebration.

Is there a "bourgeois revolution in Nicaragua?" he asked.

"No!" the crowd shouts back.

And Castro agrees. "There's no such thing as a bourgeois revolution in Nicaragua. In Nicaragua there is, in the first place, a people's revolution whose main strength is found in the workers, the peasants, the students, and the middle strata of the population."

". . . it is an historical imperative that one day we'll all be free" in Latin America that follow the Cuban, Nicaraguan, and Grenadian road.

The same message about the way forward for nations oppressed by imperialism was right in Fidel's United Nations speech last fall, a magnificent speech. Fidel told the UN General Assembly that the "prospect of a world without capitalism is not too frightening to us revolutionaries."

"If the system is socially just, the possibilities of survival and economic and social development are incomparably greater," he said. "The history of my own country provides irrefutable proof." And then he went on to list the accomplishments of the Cuban socialist revolution.

"The exploitation of the poor countries by the rich must cease," Fidel said. "I know that in many poor countries there are exploiters and those who are exploited. I address myself to the rich nations, asking them to contribute. And I address myself to the poor nations, asking them to distribute."

The line of the Cubans, the Nicaraguans, the Grenadians, is the *socialist revolution*. This, of course, doesn't entail an ounce of sectarianism toward anti-imperialist struggles that are led by non-proletarian forces or that are stopped short of full national and social liberation.

Today, Fidel understands better and explains the role of the working class in leading the revolutionary process, leading the peasants and all oppressed classes of society, all the oppressed nations of the world, to liberation.

Moreover, as Jack [Barnes] explained in his talk to the conference last week and in more detail during the discussion today, the Castro leadership increasingly explains its ideas explicitly by going back to Marx, Engels, and Lenin. Over the fall, Pathfinder will be helping to advance our discussion by beginning to make speeches by Castro available in English that none of us have had an opportunity to read.

The Castro leadership never stopped growing politically. It has not only drawn conclusions from the experiences of the international class struggle over the past decade, it has deepened its capacity to ground its analyses and explanations in the fundamental proletarian line of march developed by the Marxist movement from 1848 through the October 1917 revolution and the Communist movement under Lenin.

This is the line that the Cubans have taken into the Non-Aligned Movement. They have gone in fighting for the leadership of all those nations and all those peoples that are ground down by imperialism. From their position since September 1979 as official head of the movement for three years, they have presented an anti-imperialist alternative to those governmental figures and capitalist politicians that have traditionally predominated and conciliated with Washington.

At the Havana conference, the Cubans fought around the question of Kampuchea and against imperialist-inspired maneuvers in Indochina. The Cuban representative even called the delegate from Singapore "a dirty rat" for supporting Pol Pot. The Cubans also led the fight against the Camp David accord.

This policy has won respect, attention, and prestige for the Cuban socialist revolution among the oppressed all over the world. It has been a victory for the socialist perspective in these countries, and a lesson in how to operate in the real world, to be a revolutionary politician, to influence and attract masses of people with the prospect of world socialism.

This brings us to the point raised in the discussion about one of the banners we've displayed in the conference hall: "Workers and oppressed nations of the world unite!"—a quotation from Lenin.

The point was made by one comrade that this is not 1920, it's 1980, and the whole semicolonial world is much more proletarian and urbanized today than it was in 1920. This is true. But far from making Lenin's slogan invalid, this important change makes the slogan's implications for socialists even *more* important and timely.

The Castro leadership recognizes this. Isn't that the lesson of the revolution in Grenada? Of the powerful urban insurrections in Nicaragua? Of the role of workers in the Iranian revolution? The lesson of South Korea, of the Cordobazo in Argentina, of Chile, of what's happening today in Brazil?

Isn't it clearer than ever today that the proletariat is taking the leadership of anit-imperialist struggles, and that any current that stands back from *this* struggle is going nowhere? That's the lesson we draw from the history of the colonial revolution during the past fifteen years. And that's part of our political convergence with this current. It is part of the objective historical basis that has made possible this political convergence, that has helped settle in life questions around the *tactic* of rural guerrilla warfare, the role of the mass movement and mass organizations, the need for the Leninist-type parties.

And there will be more experiences and more lessons as imperialism grinds down the workers and the peasants of the semicolonial world, creates more of its own gravediggers, more explosions, more revolutionary opportunities.

We discussed this at our May National Committee plenum. We said that this is not a one-way convergence of this current toward the Fourth International. It's not simply a convergence in a political vacuum. It is a convergence of our world movement, our Leninist tradition, and our program with those of a current growing out of a revolutionary upsurge, and *both sides* are reacting and changing under the new world relationship of class forces, the resurgence of the world revolution, of the increasing weight of the proletariat and urban struggles in this new rise.

We're all being affected and tested. We can see those effects in the turn into the industrial working class projected at the World Congress of the Fourth International. We see it in the speeches of Castro; the statements of Sandinistas; the *Granma* interview with Humberto Ortega where he explained the rethinking the Sandinistas went through as a result of the way their revolution triumphed; and in the development of the New Jewel Movement, which we've discussed here yesterday and today.

Our goal is not to win Maurice Bishop or Fidel Castro or Daniel Ortega to affiliate to the Fourth International. That's ridiculous. We're against that. That approach to the question will get us nowhere in doing what the Fourth International was established to do and has been fighting to do for more than 40 years—to build a mass international proletarian party that can lead the world socialist revolution forward, an international based on the real traditions of Lenin and the Bolsheviks. We have the biggest opportunity ever today to move further down that road; and any formalism or sectarianism is a *road block*.

If I understood one of the comrades who spoke in the discussion, he seemed to be belittling the importance of this development by suggesting that the political level of the European working class precludes their drawing any significant political lessons from the experience of the Cuban, Nicaraguan, and Grenadian revolutions.

I think this is dead wrong. We in the SWP certainly believe it's very important for party members to go down to Cuba, to go down to Grenada, to go down to Nicaragua and to talk to the revolutionists there, including leaders of the revolution. We think it's important for all American workers to go down and learn from these revolutions. That's our approach.

Of course, there's a lot they can learn from us, too. There's a lot they can learn from us about U.S. politics, about the American working class, about revolutionary strategy in the imperialist countries. Whenever we meet these revolutionists, they want to know about politics here. They ask us questions.

Prime Minister Bishop asked Andrew, Diane, and me a

lot of questions about the American class struggle, about what is going on in the working class, how it is being affected by Carter's war propaganda. Of course, these comrades don't know as much about American politics as we do. It would be an abysmal comment on us if that weren't true! Making the American revolution is our job, not theirs.

But there's a process of discussion, a discussion that we want to become part of. And we and the rest of our class will learn and benefit from the experience of these socialist revolutions.

The Cuban working class has the highest political level of any working class in the world today. It is the most class conscious, the most internationalist. I don't think there can be any doubt about that.

So it's not only Latin American and Caribbean workers who will lean from these revolutions; European and U.S. workers will have a lot to learn too.

Now, I want to deal briefly with a couple of other questions. I'm glad Barry [Sheppard] clarified the question that came up during the discussion of whether hotel and restaurant owners are part of the Grenadian capitalist class. They certainly are. In fact, the hotel owners association is one of the backbones of the capitalist class, along with the landlords, merchants, and the few industrialists.

The New Jewel Movement is leading and organizing the Grenadian workers and peasants so that they can replace this ruling class and reorganize society on a new, nonexploitative basis, as Cuba has done.

But this is not an automatic or quick process. It requires leadership. And a big test of the NJM has been its capacity to guide the Grenadian working class and its allies through all the thickets and brambles of counterrevolution inside and outside the country, imperialism, the local bourgeoisie, the lack of experience in administering and running an economy and a government. The New Jewel Movement is educating, leading, and organizing the workers of Grenada in learning how to plan, how to govern, how to control production, how to manage.

The Grenadians, like the Cubans and Sandinistas, are continually trying to find ways to increase the involvement, the participation, and the mobilization of the workers and toilers around every big decision that faces the country.

When Cuba faces a confrontation with imperialism, what does the Castro leadership do? It mobilizes millions of people and explains the issues. What the stakes are. That times are not going to be easy. What the possible consequences are. And 5 million people turn out to say, "For sure, Fidel, give the Yankees hell!" And a few thousand head for Mariel.

In the process, the masses have been involved, they've participated, they've been educated, and their class consciousness and internationalism have been raised.

And it's by following this example that the Sandinistas and the Grenadians are advancing.

Finally, as Liam explained at the rally the other night, it's not all smooth sailing for Grenada, as the June 19 counterrevolutionary bombing shows. There will be more bombs, more attempts to crush the revolution. Counterrevolution is being organized right here on U.S. soil with the support of the U.S. government. That makes our solidarity here especially important. And we look forward to going out of this meeting, as Andrew will explain, to mount solidarity for the Grenadian revolution in this country.

We also want to work with our comrades in the Caribbean, the comrades of the GRS in Martinique and Guadeloupe, our comrades in the Dominican Republic, our Puerto Rican comrades, our Canadian and British comrades. Solidarity work in Britain and Canada is very important, because those are two of Grenada's key markets and sources of imports and countries with many West Indian workers who can be profoundly influenced by Grenada.

We also look forward to a political discussion on the enormous and historic stakes for our world movement—for the entire world working-class movement—that are posed by this revolutionary development. Along with our turn to the industrial working class, proletarianizing the sections of the Fourth International, this is at the center of world party building today.

That discussion is now beginning. And that is exactly what we want in our world movement—an open, comradely, energetic political discussion. One where we get out information and points of view as widely as possible, so we can achieve maximum clarity on this question. Because it is the *question of questions* for us—taking advantage of the opportunities to build a revolutionary working-class international.

Appendix I: (Reprint from *Intercontinental Press*, November 19, 1979.)

Interview With a Leader of the Grenada Revolution

'We Will Not Submit or Bow to American Bullying'

[The following is an interview with Selwyn Strachan, a founder and central leader of the New Jewel Movement and currently the minister of labor, works, and communications in the People's Revolutionary Government of Grenada. The interview was obtained by Ernest Harsch in St. George's, Grenada, on October 29.]

* * *

Question. The People's Revolutionary Government (PRG) calls itself a "workers government." Could you explain that?

Answer. Ever since the inception of our party, we have espoused a particular ideology—we call ourselves socialists.

Our party is committed to the task of improving the quality of life of the working people of our country. We see the workers as the revolutionary class in society, and we are determined to raise their political and ideological consciousness.

We say we are a workers government and we are determined to improve the quality of life of the worker. Whilst we recognize the importance of better wages and working conditions, we feel that it is absolutely necessary—if we want to move the struggle forward, if we want to build a workers state, if we want to build a worker-peasant state—that we devote a lot of time to the building of the political and class consciousness of the workers in our society.

And that is a very long, long task that we have. Because even at this stage in our country, the workers are not fighting for political rights. They are still at the trade-union level, for better wages and working conditions. They are not fighting for laws to protect their interests. They are not at that stage yet.

We are trying to ally the other classes in society with the workers. In other words, we see the struggle in a wider context, not just working-class struggle on behalf of workers, but linking that, trying to bring all the oppressed classes into alliance with the working class to fight for all the democratic, progressive measures at this particular stage in the struggle.

Q. Would you like to see a stage where the workers would be sufficiently politicized and class conscious to begin raising their own demands and begin mobilizing themselves, rather than waiting for the government to act?

A. I don't see spontaneous reaction. We feel that everything has to be properly guided. It should be done in an organized way, rather than allowing things to be spontaneous. Sometimes we can have that. But our aim is to organize in a serious way so that the revolution is not hampered.

In other words, we do not think that anything rash should be done now that will hold back the revolution, and in turn hamper the workers and the working people as a whole. We are against spontaneous reaction, but at the same time we are also against any kind of measure that will hold back the raising of the class consciousness of the workers.

The thing is, there are a number of stages that we have to go through. The society, we see, is predominantly petty-bourgeois. That is very deep in the country. The working class is very weak numerically.

Q. Petty-bourgeois in the sense of a strong peasantry?

A. A strong peasantry, right. And a lot of individualist activities, vendors, lots of people who are self-employed.

The peasantry is the single largest category of people in the country. It is twice as strong as the working class, maybe one-and-a-half-times stronger. And then we have all these other people around, the artisans, the fishermen, the small and medium sized businessmen, and so forth.

We feel that whilst we move rapidly to raise the consciousness of the working people, including the working class, at the same time we have to consolidate our position in certain sectors of the economy, which will again help to strengthen our position, raising the level of the productive forces.

In other words, we see us moving toward socialism, using the mixed-economy approach, the noncapitalist path at this stage. And that, of course, will help us increase the strength of the working class in our country, prepare us for the advancement to socialism, where we can eventually have the dictatorship of the proletariat.

But now it is impossible. We have to keep up the political education work. We have to do work among the workers, work among the farmers, work among the fishermen, work among the women, the youth, and even the small and medium sized businesspeople, the middle strata, and unite the population and prepare them for the next stage of the struggle.

In other words, we see this as a democratic phase of the struggle, preparing the masses for the transition to socialism.

Q. Do you see this in terms of distinct historical stages?

A. This, as we see it, is a distinct historical stage. It is the democratic process. And in the democratic process, one has to look at all these factors.

The aim, of course, is socialism. But socialism cannot just come, just so. We have to prepare the ground for that social transformation. We see it now as democratizing the society, making sure that all the rights of the working people are fully entrenched, making sure that the economy is consolidated, having a full grip on the key sectors of the economy, and increasing the overall level of productive forces, which will prepare us for the transition.

In other words, we are moving to socialism, bypassing capitalist development. So we see this as a historical stage in the development of society.

Q. How would you compare the revolutionary process here in Grenada with the development of the Cuban revolution, particularly in its early days?

A. First of all, the revolution took place in 1959 in Cuba. Ours takes place in 1979, twenty years after.

Their revolution was led by revolutionaries, just like Grenada.

Cuba, of course, was a neocolonial society, totally dominated by America. Our country was also dominated by imperialism.

The working class there was also weak, just like ours here. In other words, it was a petty-bourgeois society, like ours.

And Cuba, more or less, went through the same process that we are right now going through. What Cuba had in 1959, after the revolution, was a dictatorship of the masses, just like what we have here. They had to go through a similar process that we are in fact going through right now.

For example, in the first twenty months of the revolution, Cuba did not really get into the commanding heights of the economy, the banks, big factories, and so forth. It was after a period, they began to move into those areas. We have a similar situation here.

Of course, there is a slight difference in that we don't have any indigenous factories and enterprises like Cuba had, because they had sugar cane and mills and so forth. We don't have any factories here producing from nutmegs or cocoa or bananas. Therefore it was much easier for them to acquire these things. They didn't have to get into the whole question of industrialization from scratch, like we will have to do.

We believe that our course of development will be more or less the same as the Cuban revolution. There may be one or two minor differences, but nothing dramatic.

And that, of course, will go for almost every country in the Caribbean, because we have been underdeveloped by the imperialist world. The character of our economies is more or less the same. Jamaica, Guyana, Barbados, Trinidad, you name it, we have been plundered by the imperialist world.

If we have taken a decision to socially transform our society, and we are adopting the correct approach according to the laws of historical development, we would more or less have to go through the same process, with slight differences because of the unevenness, since some countries are more developed than the next.

But basically, the approach will be the same, if we are moving to socialism.

Q. How much of an asset do you see the existence of the Cuban workers state being for the advancement of the Grenadian revolution?

A. That is a very, very important factor, extremely important. It cannot be overemphasized.

Because we need the greatest solidarity now. It is quite clear where we are going and how we are going there. The presence of a socialist state in the region is a definite plus for us. Could you imagine if we were Cuba in 1959, a small country like ours, what we would have gone through?

Cuba's assistance in the darkest hours of the revolution has been fantastic. Although we have gotten assistance from other countries in the region, Cuba's assistance was definitive in helping to consolidate our revolution. And it will continue to be an important asset in the region.

Given our path, given our revolutionary path, the more progressive governments emerge in the Caribbean, the better for us. The more Cuban-type governments, the better for us. But of course, Cuba is the only one yet.

And I think, since there is always a possibility of destabilization, political and economic, there will always be the need for solidarity from all friends.

For example, the economic blockade that Cuba went through from 1959 to now, we could never survive that. It is quite clear, given the signs that we have been seeing, that imperialism would be prepared to put the squeeze on us. But we are confident that because of the presence of Cuba we

Ernest Harsch/IP-I
SELWYN STRACHAN

would be able to some extent to beat back some of that, though not all, because of the solidarity of Cuba in conjunction with the rest of the socialist community.

So it is, in our view, a definite plus, an asset, the presence of Cuba in the Caribbean, in terms of helping to push our revolution forward.

Q. How would you describe the New Jewel Movement?

A. As a socialist party, with the objective of bringing socialism to this country. To that end, we are engaging in concrete work amongst the masses, preparing them for that eventual goal. Our program is geared toward that.

Q. Has it always considered itself that, from its inception, or has there been a process of development?

A. It started off as what we would call a revolutionary party, a revolutionary democratic party. We never called ourselves socialist at the beginning.

The New Jewel Movement was engaged in revolutionary politics, attacking the system, trying to raise the political consciousness of the people, and—fundamentally—raising democratic issues amongst the masses and trying to get them to struggle with us for democratic rights and freedoms.

It started off on that basis. As we got more and more mature, we were able to work out a clearer ideological position. It didn't come artificially, it was as a result of struggle, in a concrete way. Over a period we were able to work out a firm and definite ideological position.

Lots of organizations started off as Black Power organizations in the Caribbean, and eventually settled down into a permanent trend. Lots of the leaders you find in the region started off as advocates of Black Power. In the early and late 1960s, the civil rights struggle in the United States and in England had some influence on the region, through people coming back home and starting off organizations. But as the struggle developed and they became more clear on the situation, they were able to settle into a permanent trend as to how society should go, what form the struggle should take.

We went through that process also.

Q. Could you explain what's been done so far since the revolution in terms of trade-union rights and the extent of unionization?

A. Since the revolution we have been able to go on a mass unionization campaign.

Never before in the history of this country was there a law on the books which gave workers a right to join the trade union of their choice and to have protection.

Within two, three weeks of the revolution, we passed a law, called the Trade Union Recognition Act, that gave workers the right to join a trade union of their choice, without being victimized, without being harassed by their employers. That law never existed on the books before.

This has helped a great deal in pushing the unionization question rapidly forward, so much so that today in Grenada almost 90 percent of the urban working class is unionized.

At the same time, we repealed all the anti-worker laws that were passed by Gairy, laws which prevented the workers from striking, taking industrial action, and so forth in the "essential services" area. We repealed those laws completely and brought back the rights of the workers.

We also repealed the Public Order Amendment Act, which prevented organizations from holding meetings and discussing their affairs. This affected the working class and the trade unions; they weren't able to hold mass meetings of the trade-union movement. That also was lifted off the backs of the working class.

So the democratic rights and freedoms of the working class and working people have been restored—and extended.

Q. Could you explain what the new Agricultural Workers Councils (AWC) is, what its role is?

A. This is an alternative to Gairy's Grenada Manual and Mental Workers Union. The AWC is designed to organize the agricultural working class, all over the country. We have had councils set up on almost every estate since the revolution, both government and private estates, with the view to drawing more and more membership into the union and to using that as a vehicle for organizing the entire agricultural working class and to raise their trade-union and class consciousness.

To build socialism, you must organize the working class properly. That has to be done. The working class cannot be loose, out there, directionless, not knowing what they're doing.

That is one reason, apart from destroying the cult of Gairyism completely by reorganizing the agricultural working class and getting them to understand the way forward.

Q. Are there any measures that have been taken specifically to try to improve the position of women workers?

A. Yes. Definitely. We have been talking quite a bit about the discrimination of women in our society. The women have been called upon over the years to do the same thing as the men, but yet men historically have been paid much more than women, because she's a woman.

We have been advocating the concept that there should be equal pay for equal work. And this has not only been words. We looked at the estate workers, for example, where you find the woman is doing the same amount of work as the man, but the man is paid maybe a dollar or two more. In some cases we have taken steps to correct that already, where the woman is getting the same pay as the man, because they're doing equal work.

What we want to see throughout the society is the involvement of women in the overall political process. It is something that we are very strong about in our party. To that end, the women's arm of our party has been organizing around the country and trying to raise the political level of the women masses, workers included. A women's desk has been opened in one of the ministries to deal with the special problems that women face in our country.

Q. Could you explain the PRG's policy toward the involvement of foreign firms in the Grenada economy?

A. We have not worked out the concrete policy on the question of foreign investment.

We know what we do not want. It is quite clear. We feel that there are certain areas in the economy where we cannot allow foreign investors to come in, like agriculture. These are basic things.

At the same time we feel we are lacking badly in technology. Any kind of foreign investment must be heavy in capital and technology that will help to advance us, not any fly-by-night operators coming just to pick up the dollar and run.

The economy is not up for sale and is not to be pillaged any more by foreign people. If anyone wants to come here and do something, it has to be in strict guidelines.

Because the economy is underdeveloped, we are not going to sit down and say that we are totally against foreign investment. We have to look at it in a principled way, and how it can best be approached.

The important thing is that once we have the industry established, we are dictating the policy, so that the country will not be exploited. That does not mean that we cannot enter into an agreement with a foreign source on particular terms and conditions to exploit a particular resource of our country, given our limited knowledge and technology.

Q. Recently, you spoke before the local Chamber of Commerce and told the members that businessmen would no longer be allowed to exploit workers. What did you mean by that?

A. This is something we are very, very strong on. What used to happen is that workers were subject to all forms of abuses, victimization, harassment, and, of course, exploitation.

Now what we have been saying to the business community is that whilst we recognize the role that they have to play in developing this country, whilst we recognize the role of the private sector and their contribution to the development of the economy, at the same time, we cannot afford to sit by and allow workers to be subjected to the same kind of exploitation they were subjected to in the past.

We feel that steps ought to be taken in order to correct these things. Workers have rights, they are human beings, therefore they ought to be treated as human beings. They are making a contribution to the society. They are selling their labor power. And that has to be respected.

At the same time, we are not advocating the whole question of indiscipline. We are not going to encourage the workers to be indisciplined, intolerant, and abusive to management. That could hamper the development of society.

But it has to be understood that the rights of workers must be respected. We pointed out to the employers very, very frankly that in a number of areas workers were being denied their fundamental rights and so forth. We are determined to break the neck of that.

Q. When a dispute does arise between workers and management, as recently at the Coca-Cola plant, what are the government's primary considerations?

A. We feel first of all that any dispute of that sort that arises should be settled in as quick a time as possible, because we take into consideration the economy. We are in a revolutionary period and any dislocation in the economy could hamper us very badly. Therefore industrial unrest is not good for the revolution at this point in time and therefore a speedy settlement of the dispute is something we are very strong on.

Now our position is that if a dispute of that sort is unnecessarily dragged on, we will have to intervene so as to effect a quick settlement. And that is what was done on the Coke factory issue, because the issue was being dragged on, mainly by management, over five weeks. In the meantime, the economy was suffering. But not only the economy. As a whole, the public was also denied the right to have a drink. More than that, the workers and their families—and that is extremely important—were denied a right to their wages and salaries, because of the senseless attitude of the employers.

Revolutionary steps had to be taken in order to effect a settlement temporarily. What has been done in that particular case is that the factory was reopened, the workers were all returned to work, and then we said to the company, let us now set up a tribunal and try to deal with this.

Now, we hope that will be a precedent to some extent. What we would like to see happen to minimize these conflicts is to have worker-management committees set up in the different work places to deal with the question of discipline and production, and the whole question of dismissals.

Dismissals have been an effective weapon of businesspeople. Why? Because they have a large pool of unemployed people out there, who are looking for work, and therefore the workers have no job security. They cannot really function properly because the tension is great. If anything happens they're dismissed, and other workers take their place.

So we had to break the neck of that.

In the case of the Coke factory, it was quite clear that the management weren't prepared to do anything to alleviate the situation. As far as they see it, they could have dragged the thing out another two years. So we had to step in, as a revolutionary government, as a government that is fighting the struggles of the working class and the working people.

It was not a question of us taking full control of the factory. It was a question of trying to get a settlement and up to now, although the factory has been run by government, the ownership still remains in the hands of W.E. Julien and Company. All we are concerned about now is getting the industrial matter settled. Once that is settled, they can continue running the factory.

We have a number of things to do. We cannot take that on now. That is for another stage in the struggle.

But at the same time, just because we intend to allow the business community to function, we are not going to sit by and allow them to abuse workers, to fire them at their own whim and fancy. The right to work is something that we are very firm on.

Q. Are there any sectors of Grenadian society that are reacting with hostility to the revolution, who feel that their interests might be threatened?

A. A very tiny, tiny minority. The big businesspeople and the reactionary types. There is a tiny handful of middle class elements, plus the reactionary-type businessmen who have reacted with hostility to the revolution, who have engaged in all kinds of rumor-mongering, lies, and destabilization tactics. We do have that element. But they are in a tiny minority.

Q. Do you see the hand of U.S. imperialism in any of this resistance within Grenada to the revolution?

A. Yes, in a very subtle way. They are not openly hostile, except in the early days when Ambassador Ortiz was here, when he actually came and tried to be rude, and said his government would view our relations with Cuba with "displeasure."

Apart from that, they have been very subtle, not openly hostile. But we are convinced and we know that they have a heavy hand in this operation that is taking place in the country. That will increase.

Even the reaction of certain countries in the Caribbean is as a result of imperialist pressure, certain countries that are making statements against the revolution. We know for a fact that the pressure is coming from imperialist sources, and American imperialism in particular.

The American State Department has recently taken a conscious decision to put the economic squeeze on Grenada. They met in a private meeting in London with two other imperialist countries. What we have been told is that the other two countries have not been fully into it, but pressure has been brought on them to put on the economic squeeze.

America itself cannot really hamper us directly by an economic squeeze, because we don't buy much things from them, and they don't buy much things from us. But they can get their imperialist allies to bring the pressure on us, those that we sell our raw materials to and buy our manufactured goods from. We buy much more from Europe and Canada than from America itself. So they will have to try to get as many of their imperialist friends to bring the squeeze on us.

Q. How serious of a threat do you think Carter's creation of a military task force for the Caribbean is to the Grenadian revolution and to the Caribbean in general?

A. We view that as a very serious threat. It is precisely because of the advent of the Grenadian revolution that Carter has seen fit at this point in time to talk about the setting up of a military task force in the region.

Talking about Soviet troops in Cuba is an excuse, really, because they know that those troops were there for quite a long time. So using it now clearly is a way of getting an excuse to step up their military activities in the region.

They still feel that the Caribbean is their backyard and that they can dictate the policies of the governments in the Caribbean. So they are not taking too kindly to the new developments that are taking place in the region, the progressive changes taking place.

They feel that the Grenada revolution would be the main force in changing the region. And the only way they can quell that is to step up their military activities with the view to frightening the people and possibly invading our country in order to turn back the revolution, because they see their economic interests being threatened in the long run.

We categorically reject the presence of any American military troops in the region. We reject it.

And we are going to be fighting, we are going to be struggling in the region, internationally, and in all forums to ensure that America withdraws its increased military presence in the region.

It is a threat to the development of the progressive struggle in the region. It is a threat to mankind's progress. We do not think that the Caribbean area should be a militarized area. We want it to be a zone of peace. We want to develop the region along peaceful lines.

And we will not submit or bow to American bullying in whatever form it takes. That is quite clear.

Q. What do you think that working people in the United States and other countries can do to best aid the struggles of their brothers and sisters here in Grenada?

A. For one, we see the waging of a very powerful campaign within America itself to try to get America to ease up on the plan that they have for the Caribbean, to keep their hands off the Caribbean territories and the revolutionary processes that are taking place.

We also believe that working people in America should pay periodic visits to the region, visit the country, see what is happening and go back and propagandize the American public on what is really taking place in the region.

We feel that a struggle similar to the anti-Vietnam-war struggle can be waged within America on the question of the Caribbean. And not only the Caribbean, but also the entire Third World countries, where struggles are taking place.

What the working people in America have to understand is that the more revolutionary changes we have in the Third World, the more the break with imperialism intensifies, the better it will be for the working people in America itself. It will help their own struggles. □

Appendix II: (Reprint from *Intercontinental Press*, August 4, 1980.)

Interview With Prime Minister Maurice Bishop

The Class Struggle in Grenada, the Caribbean, and the USA

[The following interview with Grenada's Prime Minister Maurice Bishop was conducted July 15 by Andrew Pulley, presidential candidate of the U.S. Socialist Workers Party; Steve Clark, managing editor of *Intercontinental Press/Inprecor;* and Diane Wang, a steelworker and SWP member. The three U.S. socialists were in Grenada on a fact-finding and solidarity tour.]

* * *

Andrew Pulley. What can supporters of the Grenadian revolution, antiwar activists, and Black activists in the United States do regarding the U.S. government's war drive and slander against Grenada? How can we help combat that?

Maurice Bishop. I think there are a number of areas. Certainly the question of mobilizing the population, particularly the Blacks, the deprived minorities, progressive forces, the working class, around the importance of world peace and détente. There might be some concrete ways of getting that message across. Certainly, for example, using the Vietnam experience and what it has meant concretely for people—not only for those who died, but those who are now permanently crippled or those who have come back war heroes but still cannot find jobs.

Secondly, I think it is very important to try to organize around one or two key slogans that could dramatize and really focus in a very concrete and spectacular way on this war drive. What I'm getting at is this, for example.

Everybody knows, but most people cannot quite articulate, that the reasons for war, the reasons for any war-mongering right now, have to do essentially with the developing crisis in international capitalism. The economic problems in the United States even more so.

Witness the $142 billion defense budget or whatever it is. Fifty million dollars cut back on school lunch programs. The retrenchment, the general cutback in social expenditures.

Yet at the same time, it is equally clear that while they are cutting back in those areas, they are stepping up on defense spending. And inciting the countries of NATO, for example, to do likewise.

'Let General Motors Fight'

Now it seems to us that it should be possible to get that message across in a concrete way. To point out that really what the war drive is all about is a means of the transnational corporations, the elite in America, to try to revive their super profits, which have been falling so dramatically. And the best way always of doing that is by getting a war economy moving—step up spending in armaments, step up spending in the area of the military generally.

So the slogan, for example, that makes the point: "We don't want a war. General Motors wants a war. Let General Motors go and fight." I'm saying that it should be possible to step up that kind of message in a very concrete way so that people can understand.

Because I get a feeling—certainly the last time I was in America—last year at the United Nations—that this war-mongering was beginning to seep through to the population in general to some extent. I wasn't there long enough, I didn't speak to enough people or to an especially wide cross-section to be sure that what I'm saying is right. But certainly listening to the radio, watching the television shows, and just talking to people here and there, that impression came across very strongly.

I don't think there's any need for that to happen in the United States. I certainly feel that a carefully worked-out program aimed at getting the message across that war is *not* in the interests of the American masses, that it's really only a very tiny minority who wants this war, essentially for economic reasons. Therefore, if they want the war, let them go and fight the war. Why should we go and die for them? It's not helping us.

Third, I think precisely what your party and your newspaper have been doing, and we certainly appreciate it. Focusing on the actual reality in the region and the efforts being made by progressive and revolutionary countries to try to get a better life for their people. And doing it in as concrete a way as they can, in terms of focusing on the basic needs of the population—jobs, health, housing, food, clothing. The concrete attempts to bring these about and therefore the developing perception in the minds of the Caribbean masses that this really is a way to measure progress. Not in terms of how many industries you have or how many hotels you have when the profits are going to a very tiny elite, but in terms of what benefits are truly getting to the masses.

Getting across the point, too, that there is absolutely no doubt that for all of us in the Caribbean who are trying to develop new paths and new processes, our concern is not with America. We have no axe to grind. All we want is to be able to live in peace. To have the opportunity to develop our own processes free from all forms of outside interference, from intimidation,

BISHOP: "The reasons for war . . . have to do essentially with the developing crisis in international capitalism."

from threats of invasion, from task forces and Solid Shields and whatnot. That's really all that the people of our region are asking—that it is our right to do as we wish in our own countries.

I think, as I said, that your party and your paper have certainly been making an important contribution there. And that, to us, is one very, very key area—continuing that work.

Grenada-U.S. Friendship

The fourth thing I can think of would be the question of Grenada-U.S. friendships, Cuba-U.S. friendships, Nicaragua-U.S. friendships—these societies, which exist in the case of the three particular countries I've named.

For Grenada, it's a fairly recent development, but it has begun to spread. It's gotten to the West Coast now. And I know there are plans for pushing it further along. The importance is getting, not necessarily progressive, but democratic forces in America to join organizations like that, so that they get an opportunity of learning at first hand what is really happening and give themselves the opportunity of being able to see the other side and being able to understand what the views of the people in these countries are. So that they would get a different point of view and would not have to have to continue to be saturated by the official American propaganda.

Because, again, one of the things that struck me when I was in America—I hadn't been there in two or three years—was the extent to which the news is canned, the way it's focused. If that's really all people get exposed to—the stuff you see in the *New York Times,* what you see on all the different channels and on the radio—you really have no possibility of developing a different point of view. Because it's *all* just aimed at pushing their point of view.

And these are the same people who talk of the free press, the right to have independent views so that everybody gets to hear what's happening. I mean, I can't think of a more unfree press, a more unfree media than the American media.

Pulley. One big lie that they are perpetrating right now in the United States is that Grenada is an armed camp where every single person walks around with carbines and, therefore, if you fear for your safety, you should not go there as a tourist. The truth is that we see more people armed in a two-block area of Chicago, especially policemen, than I've seen here. Do you have anything to say about this line of propaganda?

The other line is that the new international airport that you are building here is simply a military base.

What do you have to say regarding more Black people and other Americans coming down here just to see for themselves what's happening here?

Bishop. On the first question, the question of everybody walking around with guns, the island being an armed camp, civil commotion, civil war, barricades, the rest of it. Obviously that is part of the whole attempt at propaganda destabilization.

We really have been having that from day one. Obviously the aim of that is to wreck the tourists coming here, in particular. To make tourists generally afraid to come to the country. And they are really pushing that very viciously over the past sixteen months.

Within the first few weeks, they were saying that we had cut down the forests in the middle of the island, in the Grand Etang region, and had missiles aimed at neighboring islands. Then there was another story saying that we had burrowed all the earth from under the island and established pontoons and a U-2 base so that the Soviets could attack. Another one said that there was a Soviet naval base on the offshore island of Carriacou.

Obviously that kind of propaganda cannot affect our people. The island is so small that in a quarter of a second everybody knows that it's a joke and a lie. But on people outside of the country, it can obviously have an effect. And has had some impact.

It's the same with this new line about the island being an armed camp. That's just the latest round of propaganda destabilization. We've had a lot of it. They have of course been linking that to economic destabilization—attempts at wrecking the economy.

To go back to tourism again, there are two recent examples that you might find interesting. In February a hotel owner here, the owner of a hotel called the Calabash, received a letter from one of the travel agents in New York saying that the people who were booked to come down had cancelled out because the travel agency had been advised by the State Department that Grenada was off bounds. We pub-

All we want is to be free from all forms of outside interference . . .

lished that letter. The U.S. embassy, of course, denied it.

More recently still, someone did a survey for us in the Washington, D.C. area, and they discovered that of the twenty-five travel agencies *nineteen* advised against coming to Grenada, arguing that it was unsafe, the usual stuff.

So that economic destabilization has certainly continued.

As you know, they have been moving more and more now to the third leg of that system of destabilization, the violent destabilization, and more particularly to assassinations and straight terror. All of this is predictable.

'Come See For Yourself'

We would certainly see it as important for Black Americans to come down to Grenada, for the rest of Americans generally to come, members of the American working class, American working people in general to come to our country *to see for themselves.* We feel that in the final analysis that is the best proof. Don't wait and listen to the propaganda. Come down and see.

I just opened the Caricom [Caribbean Community] ministers of health conference a while back this morning. In talking to a few of the ministers right after the opening, they were all pointing out that they can't believe that they are in Grenada when they consider the propaganda that they were hearing on *all* of the radio stations, that they were reading in *all* of the national newspapers over the past few months.

One sister from Barbados was saying that two weeks ago she heard on the radio station in Barbados a report that said that the Cuban construction workers at the airport are all walking around in full jungle fatigues with AK-47's on their backs, and that government ministers are likewise walking around that way. That children eight, nine, ten, years old walk around carrying guns in the streets. That children are going to school with guns in their hands. That there was a civil war going on in the country. That a barricade had been established in one part of the island near the airport, and people were saying they would not lift the barricade until all the Cubans were sent back home and all detainees released.

Of course, all of these are figments of the imagination. And this sister from Barbados was just so glad that she was able to come herself.

So one of our main slogans has been, "Come to see for yourself." We really think that's very important. The extent to which more and more people can have the opportunity to come down and judge for themselves. We feel that's one of the very best ways of countering these attempts at propaganda destablization.

Steve Clark. What has been the response of the U.S. government to your government's request for extradition procedures for Eric Gairy?

Bishop. That has had a varied history. In the first few weeks and months before we even formally applied for the extradition, they were all giving the impression, the U.S. embassy people in Barbados, that it's a formality, a very simple matter and so forth. Then, of course, they told us that we should get down to the formal aspects of it—prepare the warrants, and the back-up witnesses, proofs, and whatnot. We did all of that.

By November, we got a written communication from them, saying that the papers were in order. No problem. Then by January they came back saying that they had discovered the papers were not in order. There is some more information they want.

In between all of that [U.S. Ambassador] Sally Shelton comes to Grenada last December, at our invitation, and her line was that America didn't want Gairy. So, we pointed out that, well then, *we* want Gairy. America doesn't want Gairy. Gairy is saying he is coming back tomorrow morning. So what's the problem. Let him come. [Laughs.]

Of course, she had no answer to that. Because obviously what was going on was just the usual hypocrisy.

More recently, in the last two or three months, they have come out publicly for the first time—not publicly, but privately to our ambassador—saying that they have lifted all surveillance on Gairy—something that they kept saying that they were doing to some extent within their limited resources and whatnot. And that, so far as they were concerned, the Gairy question was a dead letter.

So it has now come to the point where

they have admitted openly that they are not going to bother with our request for extradition.

Carter Harbors Eric Gairy

Obviously, this is going to be one of the main stumbling blocks to having any kind of reasonable relations with the United States. Because it is not possible to accept that any country, and one that deems itself to be a friendly country, has the right to harbor fugitives from justice from our country—criminals, people who are using the territory of this other country to incite aggression against our country, to actively plan counterrevolution, to plan for mercenary invasion and all that sort of thing.

Therefore, that certainly is going to be one of the major stumbling blocks to the development of any reasonable relations.

Clark. Going back to a point you made earlier. One of the slogans that very quickly has developed into probably the most popular antidraft slogan is, "We won't fight for Exxon." This relates most directly to the war dangers in the Middle East rather than in the Caribbean. But it shows the beginning development among these activists, who are the backbone of the growing antidraft movement, of a consciousness of the cause of war. In the early stages of the Vietnam War, there were many antiwar activists who thought this was just simply a mistake on the part of the U.S. policymakers. It took quite a while into the war before the consciousness of the role of big business, the consciousness that the war was being fought for a specific reason in the interests of a tiny handful, began to develop. But that's there now right at the beginning of this new fight.

Bishop. That's fantastic.

Clark. We think that another very positive thing in terms of mobilizing solidarity not only with Grenada but with Nicaragua, El Salvador, and the Cuban revolution, and against the CIA destabilization efforts in Jamaica, is the fact that Grenada is the first revolution of this power and scope in an English-speaking country with a largely Black population. So it makes it much easier for at least that segment—which is a large and important segment of the American population—to identify with the revolutions in the Caribbean and Central Ameria.

Example for U.S. Blacks

Bishop. I agree fully. I have absolutely no doubt that one of the major factors responsible for all of the aggression and hostility against the revolution in Grenada being shown by the United States government is precisely the fact that they recognize that being a small Black country, with a large Black population, and as you say English-speaking, that it becomes a lot easier for Blacks and other oppressed nationalities in the United States to identify with our goals and our aspirations. And that *must* be a real problem for them. It must be.

Because what you have in America with the Black situation is already a situation of great oppression. And they have not been able to find any solutions by the usual methods of political prisoners and continued shootings of people, like happened in Miami recently. And to have added to that the example of a Grenada-type revolution must be a frightening thing for them—particularly since they see this place as being in their backyard. And they understand only too well that more and more Blacks are going to hear about

We always try to fully involve the masses in whatever we do . . .

Grenada, about what we are trying to do. Many of them are going to join any movement that is opposed to trying to turn back our revolution.

I think your point is a key one. Extremely important.

Pulley. I'm looking forward to being able to pick up Radio Free Grenada soon in Miami.

It will be a very powerful development when its beam is strengthened, especially for the English-speaking Caribbean, of course, but also for the average person in the United States, in order to help refute all the lies. The American people are already suspicious of anything the government says about anything. Their first thought is whether the government is lying.

The more people discover that just out-and-out lies are being told about Grenada, Nicaragua, and Cuba, the more the U.S. government will have a tremendous problem trying to get away with its war drive. As people in the Black movement become aware of what your government and country is up against, they will be outraged. Because they will see it as a racist injustice, just as they have seen with regard to Haitians, the Haitian immigrants.

It was largely pressure from the Black community that forced Carter to change, at least in words, his discriminatory double-standard toward Cuban and Haitian immigrants.

A similar consciousness can be developed with regard to this revolution, the more that Black leaders, activists, and others are aware of it.

Clark. What are some of the gains of the revolution over the past year and four months that you are most pleased with? And what are the biggest challenges that you see ahead in terms of social programs and economic development and reconstruction?

Bishop. Answering that question is not the easiest thing, because people's perspectives on that really differ very dramatically.

If you went out into the countryside and you spoke to an elderly sister, her response to a question like that might be something like, "I feel free. I feel good. I feel like a Grenadian for the first time." Intangible things.

Community Mobilization

As for those of us in the party and government, our view is that the greatest single achievement, the thing that we are happiest about, is the community mobilization, community involvement, community participation. That has really impressed us most.

I can tell you, over and over again, month after month, we keep saying, "It can't continue." [Laughs.] And then month after month, you make a call and people still come out.

When the rains came in November last year, it did us tremendous damage, more than $50 million[1] worth of damage to the economy, twenty-three inches in one month. Before those rains came, there were some weekends when we'd have 85 percent of the villages around Grenada involved in community efforts. That's an extraordinary development. I tell you that in other English-speaking Caribbean countries, I don't think they'd get 2 percent of villages to be involved. And I'm not saying this in a boastful way, I'm saying it in a factual way.

In January, we closed down the schools for two weeks so as to hold seminars for all the teachers to talk about the work-study approach, curriculum reform, and so on. And during those two weeks, we asked people to organize themselves to repair, repaint, refurbish all the schools, because they were in disastrous condition. And sixty-six primary schools got refurbished and repainted in that two-week period as a result of that drive, saving the country a tremendous amout of money. Really quite extraordinary.

We see it also in the area of the village health committees that are emerging as part of our drive to move toward a primary health system. Our aim is that doctors, nurses, paramedics, and technicians working as teams will go out into the country and bring medical attention to people where they live and where they need the attention.

The disproportion in the health budget is really quite staggering. In 1978, the last year of Gairy, 70 percent of the health budget was spent on the three hospitals in Grenada and Carriacou. Those three hospi-

---

1. One East Caribbean dollar is equivalent to US$1.00.—*IP/I*

tals, in turn, attended to about 25 percent of the sick. But under Gairy only 30 percent of the health budget was spent in trying to keep together the thirty-five health centers and medical clinics around the country where the people actually went for attention.

If you understand the situation in this country in terms of poverty, in terms of the high cost of transportation, in terms of the inaccessibility of many of these health centers and medical clinics, then you can see the problem. People are sick, but they really cannot move. Even if they manage to go once, they cannot return two days later and so forth.

So we see the primary health system as being key. And getting the masses involved in that through village health committees, where they do a number of things. One, involve themselves in public health education. Two, deal with overhangings, deal with unblocking drains, which is one of the main problems with mosquitos outdoors, which means yellow fever and so on.

Third, monitoring the *quality* of health care they receive. Because doctors, naturally, came out of the system of 350 years of colonial oppression and thirty years of Gairy's misrule and neocolonialism. Their education system was preparing a tiny elite and one that was not dedicated to service but to dollar bills and to migrating as fast as they could. And even when they stayed here, they either moved into private practice altogether or insisted on their right, while being paid out of taxpayers' money, to practice privately at the same time, using hospital facilities to do so.

Now that kind of doctor is not going to join up as part of any medical team of nurses, paramedics, and technicians. So it's a real problem getting that struggle, that program going. We have been able to make some limited impact, but we have a long way to go. But we're sure it can be developed because of the community involvement and a new sense of oneness and unity in the country.

Some Concrete Benefits

The other way I think we can look at the question you asked is to try to identify a little more concretely and specifically some of the actual benefits that have come to the people. More jobs, for example, 2,500 in the first year. That has made a very small dent really in the overall unemployment rate of 50 percent, which we inherited. But obviously it has made a difference. It has helped, reduced it to about 35 percent.

Secondly, in the area of education. Before the revolution, the last year of Gairy, three students went away on university scholarships in 1978. One of the three was Gairy's daughter. After the revolution, in the first six months, 109 scholarships, 109 people are able to go abroad to study.

We've been able to reduce secondary school fees from $37 a term to $12 a term.

"The thing that we are happiest about is the community mobilization." Above, January 1980 demonstration headed by leaders of New Jewel Movement.

Next year, we intend to make it entirely free.

We have been able to increase greatly the number of scholarships in the secondary schools so that more children can get in.

We have started a breakfast and lunch feeding program in the schools so that those children who are too poor or are unable to return home for lunch will be able to keep themselves together—while your government is cutting it out.

In the area of health likewise. We inherited a situation where there were eighteen doctors working in the government service—virtually all of them concentrated in the hospitals, one or two moving around the clinics, but mostly doing a few hours every week, once a week for a few hours.

And in the first six months again, we were able to get seventeen new doctors to come to Grenada. In other words virtually the same figure as we had before were added to the system. And that has made

an enormous difference in the quality and quantity of health care available.

As you know, twelve of these seventeen doctors and dentists came from Cuba on loan to us and that, of course, has been an extremely important contribution, one of many they have made to the revolution.

So you have jobs, you have education, you have health. You also have the question of struggling with the infrastructure. Pipe-borne water has been greatly increased with the opening of the new Mardigras water project, and several others are about to be completed. That should ensure water for the whole of St. George's. There are pipes in some parts of St. George's that have not seen water for four and five years—not days or weeks, but literally four and five years, just rusted up.

We've been struggling with new feeder roads, opening the forests, for example, to get timber. Right now Grenada supplies something like 4 percent of our overall timber needs locally, when there's a lot of forest land just going idle. Without doing any great amount, just cutting a feeder road, not even paving it, just enough for a vehicle to get in using four-wheel drive, buying a sawmill for $20,000, that's all. And doing this now, we expect that in five years, we will be able to supply 90 percent of our timber needs.

There's a lot of little, relatively small things that overall have made quite an impact. These are some of the achievements.

Dependent Economy

In terms of the challenges. In a situation like ours, given our inheritance and dependent economy, we have an economy that was accustomed to looking outward for solutions never inwards toward our own needs and problems. We have a country that was misruled for so many years under colonialism and today continues to be exploited by imperialism. The inheritance, the legacy of not just waste and corruption, but of the lack of physical amenities, is really quite frightening. Three hundred and fifty years of British colonialism, for example, gave us *one* public secondary school. That's all they could build in 350 years! The other eleven were built by the churches.

When you come into that sort of situation, you obviously have to set yourself goals and targets for the revolution.

As you know, this year in Grenada is the year of education and production. And the two main things involved would be the CPE [Centre for Popular Education] and the land reform program.

The land reform commission has been established and is laying the basis for eventual agrarian reform. At this point we are mainly trying to identify the idle *lands* in the country, and to see how many of the idle *hands* are willing to work in cooperatives, so as to bring about that marriage.

Clark. And that also involves the development of a fishing industry?

Bishop. Right.

Clark. What are some of the main political features of the Grenadian revolution?

Three Pillars

Bishop. I would say that there are three main pillars of the revolution.

First, the organization and mobilization of the masses. That is very key. To always try to fully involve the masses in whatever we are trying to do, to keep them fully involved, to ensure that they understand what the problems are and where we are trying to go.

Secondly, the question of national security and defense—consolidation in those areas.

Thirdly, the question of building a sound national economy and bringing more benefits to the people, improving the quality of their lives.

Those to us are the three key pillars. And we believe that all three have to be worked on at the same time. We cannot afford to let any drop or lag behind.

In any revolutionary situation, in any progressive situation, the question of finding the right mix between the people of the country is key. The people without the guns, after all, is Allende, and we know what happened to Allende. The guns without the people, on the other hand, is Pinochet, and we know what will happen to Pinochet.

So it's a question of striking that balance, ensuring that our people understand the importance of being ready to defend our country from external attack, understand why it is that imperialism *must* attack us—why it is, therefore, that assassinations, terrorism, destabilization, mercenary invasions, *must* be a part of their agenda.

That's something that is not as easy as it sounds in our context. Generally speaking, the historical tradition of the English-speaking Caribbean has not been one of a great deal of state violence, or other forms of violence really against the people. It's much easier, I think, for people in Latin America, for example, to understand these realities.

Secondly, remembering the way we took power. While there was a long history of repression by the state, by Gairy, in the days leading up to the revolution, to some extent the people themselves were not really involved in receiving that violence on a personal level.

We don't have, in other words, a situation let's say of Nicaragua, where since 1935 people have been fighting with arms in hand from time to time to try to unseat the various Somozas.

Or a situation like Cuba. The Platt Amendment in 1902 and the constant struggle since then, year after year, the

We need to remain constantly alert, constantly vigilant . . .

years in the Sierra Maestra. You didn't have that kind of situation here.

The people's consciousness, in other words, did not come out of that objective situation that makes it fairly easy for them to understand what is possible at the hands of imperialism.

In addition, we didn't have the situation that the Cubans and Nicaraguans had, where there is a whole lot of land tied up in the latafundias, in the hands of one or two big exploiters, that you can take and just hand over, making easier the objective basis of proceeding on the subjective level. That is not our situation.

You talk about a big landowner in Grenada, you're talking about somebody with seventy-five acres of land.

So we have had right from day one this tremendous difficulty of getting across to our people, getting them to internalize in their bellies, the fact that we *are* going to be attacked, the fact that economic destabilization *is* going to continue, that the propaganda war *will* continue, that they *are* going to move eventually to assassinations and to mercenary invasions. The objective conditions for getting that message across were not there from before. People did not have that period of socialization, and therefore internalizing this was not the easiest thing.

To that extent, the recent [June 19] events, unfortunate as they are in terms of loss of life, have gone a long way towards helping to raise consciousness. Because people are now able to say, "Right. From day one the comrades were talking about that." They now see that on June 19, even while [the terrorists] moved to wipe out the entire leadership, they did it in such a way that it didn't matter that hundreds of innocent women and children could get wiped out at the same time.

That has made a qualitative difference in the people's perception of what imperialism, what counterrevolution really means.

From that point of view, it has been an extremely important experience. That certainly is one of the biggest challenges that we face, trying to get that across, trying to get our people to understand that we need to remain constantly alert, *constantly* vigilant. To understand that the threats are not there in theory, but are there in practice. We have to be ready and prepared to meet that.

You read about Allende, and you know that three months before September 11, 1973, was the last attempt on his life. So that last assassination attempt was a prelude to an actual coup. So we make the point that, in much the same way, an assassination attempt here can easily be a prelude to a mercenary invasion.

What imperialism is admitting now by moving to terror tactics and moving toward assassination attempts is that they have failed. Because all the attempts to build a popular base [for counterrevolution] have failed. Their attempts to push Winston Whyte and his so-called UPP—the United People's Party. The attempts to revive Herbert Blaize and his GNP [Grenada National Party], when the masses literally ran them off the streets; they didn't want to hear what they were saying. The attempts to use the *Torchlight*,[2] the local media, to try to assist them in their propaganda in much the same way as they used *El Mercurio* in Chile or the *Gleaner* in Jamaica.

The attempts to try to find a popular base, using elements in the country who are trying to exploit *genuine* objective grievances of the masses. In other words, conditions *are* bad. There is a lot of unem-

---

2. The *Torchlight* was a right-wing capitalist newspaper opposed to the revolution.

ployment. There is a lot of poverty. They get these people, therefore, to try to incite strikes, to try to whip up sections of the population around issues that *are* pressing issues, that we *are* concerned about, that we *are* trying to do something about. But making them at the same time feel that revolution is like instant coffee; you just throw it in a cup and it comes out presto. That you can negate 350 years of British colonialism and thirty years of imperialism and neocolonialism overnight.

A New Civilization

That is really what they have been trying to do, and they failed miserably. Even their attempts to isolate us in the region, that has been a massive failure, notwithstanding all the adverse propaganda against Grenada. While undoubtedly several *governments* are hostile—*they* didn't need propaganda to become hostile; they were hostile from day one—the *masses* in the Caribbean understand well what we're trying to do. They understand that this is a genuine process. That we are really trying to build a new process that may become a new civilization, that could have tremendous relevance as a model to their own lives.

And therefore they have not been put off, and imperialism has seen that. They have seen, too, that their attempts at economic sabotage have not bitten deep enough, partly because America is our number seven trading partner. We get virtually nothing from America in terms of our shops and stores. So they have had problems crippling us in that way.

The only option left was to move to the top of the pyramid. At the top, of course, is the terror, is the assassination, is the mercenary invasions. And I think that's one of the major challenges—getting our people to understand that. Certainly in the last four weeks, that message has gotten across a lot more quickly.

People now see the importance, for example, of joining the militia in larger numbers. The original figures relatively speaking were small; you were talking about the vanguard really in the militia. Now quite a few more thousand have joined up.

People now begin to get a deeper appreciation and understanding that really the PRA [People's Revolutionary Army] and the small militia that we had at first cannot seriously defend the country in a situation of all-out attack. That we can really only do that through a people's war, to be able to fight on that front. So that when the mercenaries are passing and they look at what appear to be innocent children and women bathing in a river, as they get going they get a bullet in their back. I think our masses are getting to understand that better now.

And a lot of that consciousness has certainly come as a result of recent events, and not just in Grenada. There are the assassinations of Archbishop [Oscar Arnulfo] Romero in El Salvador and Walter Rodney in Guyana; the destruction of the Eventide old people's home by fire in Jamaica on exactly the fourth anniversary of the similar destruction of Orange Lane in 1976[3]; the recent attempt on [Prime Minister Michael] Manley's life and the coup d'etat attempt over there. And then, of course, in Grenada, the June 19 bombing coming right after the April 26 plot.[4]

Jerry Hunnicutt/IP-I
Recent attacks have highlighted importance of revolution being able to defend itself.

When you think of it, after just fifteen months, four plots—the October plot, the November plot,[5] April 26 plot, and a few weeks later, June 19. And in each of the plots, what is central is wiping out the leadership. So I think we are beginning to get that clarity a bit more now, and that certainly has been a very important development from our point of view.

At this point, our feeling very strongly is that what is happening in Grenada is really part of a regional plan that imperialism has devised for dealing with progressive forces and revolutionary processes in the region. It's more than regional, it's clearly worldwide—the attempts to roll back the Afghanistan revolution, the continued search for bases in that area, the question of Iran and the attempts to invade that country a few months ago, the military presence in the Indian Ocean and the Persian Gulf area, the floating arsenal at Diego Garcia.

And in our own region, Carter's task force last year, Solid Shield '80 this year, artificial Cuban crisis in Peru, artificial crisis in Nicaragua over the two members of the junta who resigned, continuing destabilization attempts in Jamaica. The pattern is quite clear.

Cuba in the Vanguard

We feel that there are a series of concentric circles that imperialism has drawn up.

Into their first circle they have certainly put Cuba, Nicaragua, and Grenada as being the key countries to get at.

Cuba for obvious reasons. It is obviously the vanguard in this region.

Nicaragua because of its *tremendous* importance for Central America. Everybody in Central America wants to be a Sandinista. It's a massive problem there for them.

Grenada because of our powerful potential example for the English-speaking Caribbean countries, and indeed for the French- and Dutch-speaking Caribbean countries. So that's their first circle.

In the second circle we believe they have countries like Jamaica, Guyana, St. Lucia, Surinam, El Salvador. Countries where either there have been positive developments on the anti-imperialist front, or where there have been important attempts at building new structures for the people and bringing new benefits, or where there are important progressive forces in opposition or in power who are determined to bring about these changes.

Or where, as in the case of El Salvador, there is an ongoing national liberation struggle that clearly will not be settled in any reformist way. All attempts at reformism in El Salvador *must* fail.

Their third circle, therefore, will be aimed largely at all progressive forces, individually and collectively, whether in or out of office. That would explain, for example, the Rodney slaying or the Archbishop Romero slaying. They understand the potential that the left-progressive forces in the region have, and they are determined to crush that potential, using assassinations.

So it's an extremely dangerous period for us in this region.

Artificial Cuba Crisis

Clark. The U.S. propaganda around the Cuban emigrants has backfired on Carter, especially following the opening of the port of Mariel, the massive anti-imperialist marches in Cuba, and the racist treatment

---

3. In May 1976, at a time of U.S.-backed destabilization efforts against the Jamaican regime, fifty armed men attacked a tenement section in central Kingston that was a stronghold of Michael Manley's People's National Party. They set fire to it, killing ten persons. Four years later, in May 1980, a similar fire was set at the Eventide nursing home in Kingston, killing 144 elderly women.

4. In late April 1980, Kennedy Budhlall—an opponent of the revolution and a large-scale marijuana trader—was arrested along with several others for planning to overthrow the government on April 26. The plotters had several supporters at one army camp.

5. In late October and early November 1979, a number of counterrevolutionaries were arrested on charges of plotting to overthrow the government, including Winston Whyte, former head of the right-wing United People's Party; Rupert Japal of the bourgeois Grenada National Party; and Wilton De Ravinere, a former police corporal.

of the Cubans in the United States. What was the impact here in the Caribbean?

Bishop. Was it in the *Militant* that I saw the Fidel interview with Lee Lockwood from way back in 1965? Did you repeat that in the paper? [See April 18, 1980, *Militant.*] That I found to be an extremely important interview, particularly as it was fifteen years old, in tracing the history of this whole emigration question.

It was really quite succinct, the way Fidel put it. Pointing out that from the word *go* it was an artificial crisis being created. That people, of course, when they were able to leave freely were leaving freely, nobody was blocking them. It became more convenient eventually for the Americans to force them to escape and then treat them as heroes, so that they can get propaganda out of it.

In South Africa, there are millions of Blacks being kept as hostages. Yet they are making so much fuss about fifty-three American hostages . . .

It was really quite an important article, coming at the time it did, especially as it was done such a long time ago.

That propaganda has really done damage, there's no question about it, in the English Caribbean. Given that there's all this talk about "boat people running from Communism" and so forth. I think a lot of the Caribbean masses have had difficulty in comprehending what is really happening and putting it in a full context.

Because what's the reality? If any of those islands had America's doors opened tomorrow morning, there would be six people left on the island. That's the reality. But they make this song and dance.

The imperialist-controlled media have the resources, they have the skills, everything else. We find that there has been a marked improvement in imperialist propaganda throughout 1980 on virtually every issue. First of all, the speed with which they respond and the amount of ammunition they throw into it has been quite extraordinary.

Consider Afghanistan, in December of last year. Just think of the speed with which they moved and how quick that propaganda built up and therefore how difficult it was to combat and counter it.

But really on every issue. Within seconds of the bomb attack here in Queen's Park, the United States embassy in Bridgetown [Barbados] was already sending reports out. Interestingly, their first reports were saying that members of the leadership had been killed. Very interesting. We want to know, how did they know that?

Or take Iran, the question of these fifty-three hostages. Again, the speed they moved on that question, and the amount of support they were able to muster, made it difficult for people to put it in a full context in terms of the twenty-seven years of oppression under the shah, armed by American guns, and the very deep feelings of indignation as a result of all that by the people of Iran. The feeling that if America is harboring this man, then what is required?

But even more fundamentally, the fact that you have a situation like in South Africa, where there are millions of Blacks being kept as hostages. Yet here they are making so much fuss about fifty-three hostages. Millions of African hostages, imprisoned in a system of apartheid. That's not important. You never hear talk of sanctions about that, but they want sanctions for fifty-three.

It's difficult, because they come over with this powerful emotive line. They put it in the context of the need for international security of all embassies. And it leads many democratic, even some progressive countries to take a firm position against—without ever putting it in any kind of context.

Pulley. One thing that has hurt the imperialists in their drive against Iran has been the attitudes of a good number of the parents of some hostages. Many have come out against the U.S. raid, against the sanctions. A majority favor what Carter is doing, but it's certainly a large number who are vocal and are opposed to it.

They're having a rough time. They've been forced to back away from what was the case at the time of the raid in April, when it looked like imminent war. Everything blew up in their face.

Bishop. The OPEC countries came out with a very strong statement in the last two days. Really good news. I think it was the day before yesterday. Threatening an oil boycott.

Clark: Fidel had urged that in his May Day speech.

Bishop: That's right. That was a first-class speech. It really came over powerfully. What was important to me about that whole trip was the very, very close feelings between the Cuban people and their leader. That was extraordinary. It took Fidel about ten minutes before he could open his mouth. Everytime he tried to say something, the people just kept going again. I really found that extraordinary, because you're talking about a million and a quarter people or whatever it was.

And at the end, their tremendous discipline was another eye opener. Whole waves of people moved to the left while others stood still, moved to the right while others stood still. Then the front rows moved out by a few hundred thousand, the back rows by a few hundred thousand. Whole waves of people, left and right, left and right, no pushing. And in ten or fifteen minutes, that square was empty. An extraordinary manifestation of discipline.

Diane Wang. Even the *New York Times* had to comment on that. They wrote with a great deal of consternation about that rally. They had to admit not only the enthusiasm, but the discipline.

Bishop. Yes, it was so striking. You would have had to write your article on the plane before you got there really—which they do sometimes.

Clark. The lies on Afghanistan are often particularly outlandish because it is so geographically remote. The media at one point recently were reporting that an army of 20,000 guerrillas—they always call them "Muslim freedom fighters," failing to point out that there are Muslims on both sides—were surrounding Kabul. But then a few days later, if you turned to the bottom of a remote page, you noticed a little item saying the story turned out not to be true.

One of the things we try to do with the *Militant* and *Intercontinental Press/Inprecor* is simply to counteract the barrage of lies, just to keep reminding people that the capitalist press will stoop to outright deception. Lenin said that they often tell the truth in the little things so that they can lie in the big ones.

Bishop. On the Afghanistan question, we have been pointing out here in Grenada that what we are really concerned with there was the April 1978 revolution, not so much the December 1979 events. And in the intervening eighteen months, what was happening—in terms of the attempts at destabilization, the armed attacks from Pakistan and elsewhere, the plans of imperialism. And that what requires solidarity and support, therefore, is the right of the

We have nothing at all against the people of America. Our quarrel is with the system of imperialism . . .

people of Afghanistan to build their revolution. And people can relate to that over here, because they see it happening to us too. They know we can have a similar type problem.

Clark. One last question. What would you like to say to working people in the United States? To the Black community in the United States? What message would you like us to take back?

Bishop. First of all, we would like to stress something that imperialism has been trying to use as a means of dividing and ruling—and that is that we have absolutely no quarrel with the American people. We have nothing at all against the people of America as a people.

Our quarrel is with the system of imperialism. Our quarrel, therefore, is with the American establishment and all its various manifestations—whether it's through the presidency or National Security Council or the State Department or the CIA or the powerful business lobby or the powerful media or whatever. That is who our quarrel is with. And particularly insofar as that establishment seeks to support by violence the right of their transnational corporations to continue to exploit and rape our resources. That is what our quarrel is with.

After all, more Americans come to our country every year than the entire population of Grenada—140,000 came by ship last year, and I'm not talking about those who came for stay-overs.

So that is not our quarrel and we want to make that clear. Because imperialism has been doing its best to try to sow all sorts of confusion in that area.

Likewise, when you come to the question of the Blacks and other oppressed minorities in America, obviously we have a particularly close feeling, given our own cultural background and our own history. There is a very close sense of cultural identity, which the people of Grenada automatically feel for American Blacks and which we have no doubt is reciprocated by the American Black community.

Because our own struggle is internationalist, we have over the years been giving our fullest support to all international causes that demand such support. We see that as our internationalist duty.

Since the revolution, we have continued in that vein. We were the first country in the Western Hemisphere to recognize the Polisario Front; the second country in the world to recognize the provisional junta in Nicaragua on May 23 last year, fully three weeks before they finally won their victory; our open and consistent support to the PLO, for Puerto Rican independence, and so forth. That is our position.

And therefore we see the importance of progressive forces worldwide joining together. We see that struggle as being *one* struggle, indivisible. And what happens in Grenada, we recognize its importance for all struggles around the world. And therefore we're willing to support any of the struggles around the world. And we feel that on that basis, the progressive forces and democratic forces in America ought to give their support to our revolution also.

We certainly place a great deal of importance on the activity, the potential, and the possibilities for the American working-class movement. Both in terms of mobilizing and organizing to stop any draft movement, and in terms of the potential of doing mortal damage to the international capitalist and imperialist system from within the belly of the main imperialist power on earth.

And thirdly, in terms of the great possibilities for expressing solidarity with the revolutionary struggles around the world. Something they have done before and can do again. For example, mobilizing and organizing themselves to refuse to load ships heading for particular areas.

So, our basic message would be to get across this sense: That what we are struggling against is the system of imperialism. That we have the greatest respect for the people of America. That we feel a particularly close affinity to American Blacks and other oppressed minorities, to the working-class movement in America, toward progressive forces in America. That we certainly are willing to extend our solidarity with them in their struggles, and we cer-

We place a great importance on the activity, potential, and possibilities for the American working-class movement . . .

tainly would hope that they would extend their own solidarity to us in our struggle.

Finally, our message would be: We would love to see them. We believe that it is very important that instead of reading the propaganda that is being circulated in America, they should come out to Grenada, come out to Cuba, come out to Nicaragua, and see for themselves. So that they can understand what is happening and as a result be in a better position to appreciate what is going on in this part of the world.

Let me add just one final thing. That is to say that we, without intending to be disrespectful, would very strongly recommend to the Black movement in America the importance of developing the firmest and closest links with the white working-class movement and the white progressive movement. Our feeling certainly is that in order to win that struggle inside of America, it's extremely important that all progressive forces get together and wage a consistent fight against the real enemy. Don't spend time fighting each other, debating trivialities. That's something I think is important and that I would like to get across in the message. □

Clark, Bishop, and Pulley during interview

Diane Wang/IP-I

Appendix III: (Reprint from *Intercontinental Press*, September 8, 1980.)

Interview With Revolutionist From Martinique

The Struggle Against French Colonialism in the Caribbean

[Although the Caribbean has been undergoing a process of radicalization in recent years—a trend seen most clearly in the victory of the Grenada revolution in 1979—the English-language press has had little coverage of developments on Martinique and Guadeloupe, two French-speaking islands in the Lesser Antilles.

In August, *Intercontinental Press/Inprecor* talked with Gilbert Pago about the situation in those islands and about the impact of the Grenada revolution. Pago is a leader of the Groupe Révolution Socialiste (GRS—Socialist Revolution Group), the Antilles section of the Fourth International.]

* * *

Question. Could you give us some background information about Martinique and Guadeloupe?

Answer. Martinique and Guadeloupe are two small islands ruled directly from France. Between them they have a territory of about 2,700 square kilometers and a total population of some 700,000. There are another 400,000 islanders who have been forced to emigrate to France in search of work.

At one time the French colonial empire in the Western Hemisphere included Quebec, Louisiana, Haiti, Tobago, Grenada, St. Lucia, St. Vincent, Dominica, "French" Guiana, St. Pierre, Miquelon, Martinique, and Guadeloupe. Today only Martinique, Guadeloupe, Guiana, and the tiny islands of St. Pierre and Miquelon off the south coast of Newfoundland, Canada, remain in French hands.

After World War II, Martinique and Guadeloupe were made "overseas departments" of France. In theory they have the same status as any of the departments of France itself.

Each island is governed by a prefect from France who has all the real power. The local assemblies on each island have no say whatsoever over major political questions. Their sole function is to distribute the departmental budget from France.

Q. How has the status of overseas departments changed the situation in the Antilles?

A. Becoming departments of France has created a whole new set of contradictions for the islands. Today the population has the same duties as in France, such as paying taxes. But we do not receive the same benefits. For example, social security benefits are lower than in France, not to speak of wages.

Governing the islands as overseas departments and regarding the Antilles as "tropical Europe" does not change the reality that France is an industrialized country while the Antilles are underdeveloped and dominated. Some of the attempts to rule the Antilles in exactly the same way as metropolitan France have ludicrous results.

For example, each town in the Antilles gets an annual appropriation from France for snow removal. Of course, since it never snows, the appropriation is never used and is returned to France at the end of the year.

Similarly, every school budget includes an appropriation for heating the school in winter. Our children get the same "snow holidays" as children in France.

In our schools the children learn nothing about the history of the Antilles, but they do learn about "our ancestors the Gauls."

Our radio and television broadcasts come straight from France and have no Antilles character whatsoever. You turn on the radio and hear the announcer say "last night it snowed heavily," which has nothing to do with your reality. But you never hear Antillean music on the radio.

Another effect of the "departmentalization" process has been a big increase in the presence of French corporations in the Antilles. The French government's investments on the islands have been made for the benefit of the big French corporations, which send all their profits back to France, rather than using them for the local inhabitants.

In the sugar industry, which is the basis of the economies of Martinique and Guadeloupe, there are government subsidies for cane production. But all sugar refining is done in France, and then some refined sugar is sent back to the Antilles for local consumption. But the fact that it is refined in France means that it becomes too expensive for many people to buy. This also cuts the possibility of creating industries based on refined sugar on the islands.

If that were not bad enough, when sugar prices fall too low, production is cut back in the Antilles in order not to jeopardize the income of French sugar beet growers. This has a devastating effect on the islands.

The French government places no emphasis on basic food production. The result is that virtually all the daily food of the population is imported from France, which results in extremely high prices for the local population.

There has also been a big increase in investment in the tourist industry, which caters to wealthy Europeans and North Americans. But here too the industry is dominated by French companies and the profits return to France rather than remaining on the islands.

The presence of all this French investment has tended to undercut the economic power of the local white- and mulatto-owned businesses, many of which have been forced into bankruptcy. In order to survive, the local business interests had to agree to become junior partners with French capital, in return for which they are allowed to retain their political power on the islands. Many of the local businessmen have been transformed into agents of the French corporations, selling French goods, becoming managers of French property, and so on.

Another very important effect of making Guadeloupe and Martinique into overseas departments has been the huge growth in the French civil service on the islands. The government bureaucracy has been swelled by 20,000 civil servants from France, who together with their families have a big impact on the Antilles.

These government workers receive a much higher salary than the Antillean working class and they get special benefits such as six months vacation in France every two years. They therefore constitute a social base favoring the maintenance of French rule.

At the same time, the influx of civil servants from France has had a very negative effect on the employment of local people in fields outside the government as well. For example, most of the better jobs in the French-owned supermarkets, tourist restaurants, hotels, and so forth are taken by the wives of civil servants from France.

Q. What is the situation of the workers movement on Guadeloupe and Martinique?

A. Before describing the current situation, I think it would be worthwhile to describe the history of workers' struggles in the Antilles.

The class struggle had its origins in the slave revolts that rocked the islands in the nineteenth century. Between 1815 and 1848, for example, there were more than a dozen slave insurrections in Martinique and Guadeloupe.

The slave insurrection of May 22, 1848, was, in fact, successful and led the Second Republic of France to ratify the abolition of slavery. The former slaves then became a mass of peasants. But they still faced problems of racism and continuous attempts by the former slave owners to reinstitute a situation of virtual slavery. In September 1870 there was another big insurrection over those very issues.

The early labor movement on the islands was strongly influenced by this radical tradition. The first union struggles broke out in the late nineteenth century and adopted many of the traditional methods of struggle of the slaves. Early trade-unionists did things like setting the plantations and the houses of the masters to the torch, marching from plantation to plantation across the country to gain the support of other workers, and so on.

It was in the same period that the first socialist ideas appeared on the islands, brought in by reformists of the Second International.

These Social Democrats developed some influence in the labor movement. But their main orientation was to use the mass of Black workers to back up the demands of mulattos in Martinique and Guadeloupe for more access to the political and economic control over the islands that was exercised by the white descendants of former slaveowners, who comprise 4 percent of the population.

The Social Democrats and mulattos looked to France to help them fight the power of the local ruling class, and they have traditionally pushed for "assimilation" into French society and for Martinique and Guadeloupe to become Overseas Departments.

As a result, the labor movement was never concretely linked to the struggle for independence from France.

So what is the situation today? Because of the huge levels of unemployment, reaching 45 percent of the labor force, workers who have a job in the industrial, commercial, or tourist sectors of the economy are considered very lucky, even though they are paid far less then they would get for the same work in France.

This heavy unemployment and low wages explain why the more skilled workers tend to emigrate to France.

Labor struggles generally focus on protecting jobs and fighting for a living wage. There have been big fights recently in the construction industry, among dock workers, in the shopping centers, hospitals, and among municipal workers.

There has, however, been little experience in Martinique and Guadeloupe with political strikes. This is due to the strength of the reformist trade-union leaders (Stalinists as well as Social Democrats) and the relatively weak level of revolutionary national consciousness.

Q. How big is the union movement in Martinique and Guadeloupe?

A. Union membership tends to fluctuate quite a bit. Most workers do not maintain regular membership in unions. Participation rises sharply during strikes and then falls sharply again when the strikes are settled. So it is hard to give absolute figures.

But there is big sympathy with the unions. During last April's strike, for example, about 10,000 workers marched in the streets in Martinique, which is a large proportion of the 25,000-30,000 workers on the island.

One of the problems is that the unemployed are not involved in the union movement. The GRS is waging a fight for the right of the unemployed to participate in the unions.

The biggest union federation is the General Confederation of Labor (CGT). The CGT is much more dominant in the labor movement in the Antilles than it is in France. The other union federations that exist in France, such as the French Democratic Confederation of Labor (CFDT) and Labor Force (FO), have very little influence in Martinique and Guadeloupe. Unions that are not in the CGT are usually purely Antillean unions with no ties to any federation.

Q. What are the main forces on the left in the Antilles?

A. Each of the islands has its own Communist Party, and their influence in the CGT is very strong. The CPs have a long tradition in the Antilles. In fact, the CP of Guadeloupe claims to be the oldest in the Western Hemisphere, and there has been a weekly CP paper in Martinique since 1920.

The Stalinists have traditionally favored assimilation and "departmentalization." Today they remain opposed to independence, although significant pro-independence wings are developing within those parties.

In contrast to France, we do not have big Social Democratic formations. Although Social Democrats have had a presence in the trade-union movement, their past collaboration with the ruling class has been so obvious that they have lost a lot of their influence in the more militant unions.

French police in Antilles. An example of direct rule from Paris over "tropical Europe."

In addition to these forces, there is a new tendency that could best be described as "populist." This current has a very strong nationalist line, but is confused on the question of independence for the Antilles.

The "populist" tendency focuses on cultural questions and bases itself on the concept of "Négritude" espoused by the famous Antillean poet Aimé Cesaire. Cesaire, in addition to being one of the most famous poets of the French-speaking world, is also the mayor of Fort-de-France, the capital of Martinique, and is undoubtedly the most popular politician in the Antilles.

Cesaire calls for autonomy for the Antilles, but a significant wing of his party favors independence.

There are also a number of militant left parties in Martinique and Guadeloupe. Although they have had to confront powerful and well-organized reformist forces in the labor movement, their influence is growing steadily.

The militant left in the Antilles grew up under the impact of international and local struggles. Among the international struggles that encouraged its growth were the independence struggles in other French colonies such as Algeria and Indochina, the impact of the Cuban revolution, and the May 1968 general strike in France.

A new generation of fighters has also emerged from the struggles against the plunder of the Antilles by the French colonialists.

For a whole period the Maoist groupings have been the largest. But they are in a severe crisis, which stems from the crisis of Stalinism in China itself. Some former Maoists have been moving closer toward "bourgeois nationalist" forces. In Guadeloupe, for example, they have a well-organized group that leads unions with considerable influence.

In Martinique the Maoists have turned toward economist populism. They are organized in the "La Parole au Peuple" (Let the People Speak) group.

Our organization, the Groupe Révolution Socialiste, was founded by some leaders who were expelled from the Communist Party of Martinique in 1969 for "Guevarism." These leaders had a following among high school students and important sectors of the working class.

When the GRS was founded in 1971-1972, it was not yet Trotskyist. Following a long internal debate on which political road to follow, the first congress of the GRS in December 1973 decided to seek membership in the Fourth International.

Our organization has about 100 members and a substantial number of sympathizers. The largest number are in Martinique, but the branch in Guadeloupe is very good, being totally made up of union activists.

In the past few years we had some problems that resulted in some losses, but now we have begun to grow again, especially since the April strike.

In fact, in the April strike, out of the 10,000 who marched in the union demonstration, the GRS contingent was 2,000-3,000. Our slogans included "French Troops Out of the Islands!" and "Hands Off Grenada!" And GRS members presided over the meetings held after the strike.

Another group, Combat Ouvrier, also calls itself Trotskyist. It was set up in 1972 by Antillean supporters of the Lutte Ouvrière group in France. Combat Ouvrier is stronger in Guadeloupe than in Martinique.

Q. What has been the impact of the Grenada revolution on Martinique and Guadeloupe?

A. The Grenada revolution has had a big impact throughout the Lesser Antilles. As soon as the New Jewel Movement overthrew the dictator Gairy there were demonstrations on all the islands, organized by left groups, demanding recognition of the new government. For the first fifteen days not a single government in the region recognized Maurice Bishop's government.

In Dominica, where there was a dictator like Gairy—Patrick John—he responded to the demonstrations by outlawing publications and demonstrations. This was answered by a general strike, which succeeded in overthrowing the dictatorship.

In St. Lucia the left wing of the Labour Party campaigned in the July 1979 general election around the slogan of "Solidarity with Grenada." The Labour Party as a whole won 12 out of 18 seats, and the left wing won 7 of those. But now the right wing of the Labour Party is working with the conservatives to prevent the left wing from gaining control of the government.

In Martinique and Guadeloupe, Grenada had less of an initial impact than on some other islands, due to the language barrier. In addition, the GRS was the only organization that worked to organize a solidarity campaign with Grenada.

We believe that the Grenada revolution can have a very big impact on Guadeloupe and Martinique in the future. To understand the full impact, we have to look at the French arguments against independence for the Antilles, and how the experience of Grenada directly answers those arguments.

Today, as the world capitalist economic crisis worsens, it is becoming increasingly clear to people that the policy of assimilation with France has failed to solve the basic problems of the workers in the Antilles. Assimilation has not provided jobs, a decent standard of living, or ended injustice or inequality.

As a result, ever larger sectors of the population are looking toward autonomy or independence. The French rulers try to counter this trend by continually stressing four points:

First, they argue that independence for such tiny territories will result in a decline in the standard of living to the level of Haiti or some other islands. Of course they neglect to mention that the governments of these islands remain puppets of imperialism.

Their second argument is that since Martinique and Guadeloupe are so small, they would simply be swallowed up by some other imperialist power. The French add that U.S. imperialism would step in if there was any attempt to carry out a social transformation like in Cuba.

The third French argument is that the islands do not have sufficient economic resources to allow for economic growth.

And the final argument is that independence would mean an end to French economic aid and to the whole social security system, as well as an end to the possibility to emigrate to France to find work.

These arguments have an impact. People worry that independence would result in a decline in the already low standard of living. The arguments hold special sway among the older sections of the population.

But the events in Grenada are a very powerful concrete example that will help us cut through these French arguments. Grenada is only 200 kilometers from Martinique. It has a Black population and a similar history. And many of the older generation in Grenada still speak French Creole.

So we can point to Grenada as an example of what an independent country—which is not a puppet of the imperialists—can do. This island, whose population and size are much smaller than Martinique and Guadeloupe, is defying imperialism and is attacking the causes of poverty.

Grenada is the *only* island in the Caribbean—except, of course, Cuba—that has been able to create new jobs in the last eighteen months. Grenada is the only island to have lowered the prices on sugar, rice, gas, bread, and other consumer goods. It is the only island where they have been able to decrease imports by stimulating local production.

We believe that the Grenadian example can and will inspire the struggle of the workers of Martinique and Guadeloupe.

Already the French colonial government is blaming Fidel Castro and Maurice Bishop for fomenting strikes in Martinique and accuses Cuba and Grenada of intervening in the "internal affairs of France"!

Meanwhile, France has increased its troop strength in the Antilles to 16,000, which is a huge number considering the size of the islands.

These troops are not simply in the An-

tilles to deal with potential unrest in Martinique and Guadeloupe. You don't need 16,000 troops for that. They are there as part of the imperialist threat against the upsurge of revolutionary struggle throughout the Caribbean and Central America; they are aimed as much against the Grenada revolution as against the French Antilles.

The GRS has responded by organizing meetings and other activities demanding the withdrawal of French troops and hands off Grenada.

We feel that concrete solidarity campaigns organized in the Antilles labor movement to support and defend the Grenada revolution and the revolution throughout the Caribbean will help Martinique and Guadeloupe move toward independence and socialism.

Q. What kind of contact do you have with other left groups in the Caribbean?

A. We have quite a lot of contact with groups in Dominica, Antigua, Monserrat, St. Lucia, Grenada, and other islands. In 1974-75 we helped organize a defense campaign for Desmond Trotter, a political activist who was facing the death penalty on Dominica. This campaign was active on all the islands, including Trinidad. In 1975 we found a lawyer for Desmond Trotter. That lawyer was Maurice Bishop, whom I first met in Barbados in 1975 in connection with that campaign.

I should mention that the French, British, and Canadian sections of the Fourth International and the Socialist Workers Party in the United States also participated in the international campaign to save Desmond Trotter's life.

This campaign was successful, and during last year's general strike Trotter was freed from prison.

Two days after the Grenada revolution, I visited Grenada. Since then I have been back several times to follow the progress of the revolution, and other GRS members have also visited Grenada.

Another example of the kind of solidarity work we do was our activity in support of the general strike in Dominica. The GRS was active in organizing solidarity work in Martinique and Guadeloupe. Through fishermen we were able to send the strikers food, megaphones, and other supplies.

In connection with this campaign, many members of the GRS were arrested by the colonial government for participating in demonstrations, participating in an occupation of the radio station, and so on. These trials are coming up soon.

We feel that by having a strong section in the Antilles, the Fourth International has an important opportunity to participate in the Caribbean revolution in a big way. □

$12 $15 $20

Three books to be read as one . . .

about building a party that's working class in program, composition, and action. One that recognizes, in word and deed, the most revolutionary fact of our time . . .

. . . that working people have the power to create a different world as we act together to defend our own class interests—not those of the privileged classes who exploit our labor, not of those who fear us as "deplorables," or just plain "trash."

As we advance along a revolutionary course toward workers power, we will transform ourselves and awaken to our own worth. Also in Spanish and French.

The Turn to Industry and
Tribunes of the People and the Trade Unions
$20

Either book plus **Malcolm X, Black Liberation, and the Road to Workers Power**
$25

Special Offer! All three $30

WWW.PATHFINDERPRESS.COM

EXPAND YOUR REVOLUTIONARY LIBRARY

Labor, Nature, and the Evolution of Humanity
The Long View of History
FREDERICK ENGELS, KARL MARX, GEORGE NOVACK, MARY-ALICE WATERS

Why is it important to know that social labor, transforming nature, has been the motor force of humanity's evolution for millions of years? Because without that knowledge, working people are unable to see beyond the capitalist epoch, beyond the class exploitation that warps all human relations, ideas, and values. The dictatorship of capital had a beginning . . . and it will have an end. But only the revolutionary conquest of state power by the working class can open the door to a world free of capitalism's dog-eat-dog social reality. A world built on human solidarity. A socialist world. $12. Also in Spanish and French.

Thomas Sankara Speaks
The Burkina Faso Revolution, 1983–87

Under Sankara's guidance, Burkina Faso's revolutionary government led peasants, workers, women, and youth to expand literacy; to sink wells, plant trees, erect housing; to combat women's oppression; to carry out land reform; to join others worldwide to free themselves from the imperialist yoke. $20. Also in French.

Women in Cuba: The Making of a Revolution Within the Revolution
VILMA ESPÍN, ASELA DE LOS SANTOS, YOLANDA FERRER

The integration of women in the ranks and leadership of the Cuban Revolution was intertwined with the proletarian course of the leadership of the revolution from the start. This is the story of that revolution and how it transformed the women and men who made it. $17. Also in Spanish, Farsi, and Greek.

America's Revolutionary Heritage
Marxist Essays
GEORGE NOVACK

A materialist explanation of the American Revolution, Civil War and Radical Reconstruction, genocide against the Indians, rise of American imperialism, first wave of the fight for women's rights, and more. $23

Maurice Bishop Speaks
The Grenada Revolution and Its Overthrow, 1979–83

The triumph of the 1979 revolution in the Caribbean island of Grenada under the leadership of Maurice Bishop gave hope to millions throughout the Americas. Invaluable lessons from the workers and farmers government destroyed by a Stalinist-led counterrevolution in 1983. $20

FBI on Trial
The Victory in the Socialist Workers Party Suit against Government Spying
MARGARET JAYKO

The record of an historic victory in the fight for political rights, including the 1986 federal court ruling against government spying and excerpts from trial testimony by SWP leaders Farrell Dobbs and Jack Barnes. $17

By Any Means Necessary
MALCOLM X

"The imperialists know the only way you will voluntarily turn to the fox is to show you a wolf." In eleven speeches and interviews, Malcolm X presents a revolutionary alternative to this reformist trap, taking up political alliances, women's rights, US intervention in the Congo and Vietnam, capitalism and socialism, and more. $15

Lenin's Final Fight
Speeches and Writings, 1922–23
V.I. LENIN

In 1922 and 1923, V.I. Lenin, central leader of the world's first socialist revolution, waged what was to be his last political battle—one that was lost following his death. At stake was whether that revolution, and the international communist movement it led, would remain on the revolutionary proletarian course that brought workers and peasants to power in October 1917. $17. Also in Spanish, Farsi, and Greek.